STUDIES IN MODERN EUROPEAN
LITERATURE AND THOUGHT

General Editor
ERICH HELLER
Professor of German
in the University College of Swansea

ANDRE MALRAUX

ANDRE
MALRAUX

BY

GEOFFREY H. HARTMAN

BOWES & BOWES
LONDON

CONTENTS

To

HENRI PEYRE

Friend and Critic

Prefatory Note

To know Malraux, if only through his writings, is to be convinced that the universal man still exists, despite that headlong, dehumanizing tempo of events which few have felt and expressed more deeply than Malraux himself. His life appears, first of all, as a succession of adventures: but each experience has become an act of witness, and his work stands today as the literary conscience of almost every great upheaval of recent times. He is said to have spent the years 1925–27 with the Kuomintang in Indo-China and Canton. In 1934 he led, together with Gide, the protest against Hitler's counterfeit accusation of Thaelmann and Dimitroff. He saw action with a squadron of combat planes in the Spanish Civil War; when the Second World War broke out he joined the tank corps as a private and, at its end, commanded a brigade of the Maquis. As a strong if independent spokesman for the Left he raised the journalistic and political novel to eminence: today he is a member of de Gaulle's cabinet and a foremost writer on art. There is no need to emphasize here Malraux's personal courage; but it is surely a sign of such courage and of deep intellectual persistence to trust one's mind as the measure of all those rapid political and cultural changes that seem to mock the possibility of firm human comprehension.

This little volume suffers, doubtless, from many omissions, and I regret not being able to treat Malraux's political thought more directly. The few pages of comment at the end may perhaps serve as a tentative and elementary start; but already a close reading of his novels will show that Malraux was one of the first to emphasize the dictatorship of the propagandists, and to consider art and the heritage of Western culture as very special weapons in an era of ideological warfare.

I want to thank René Wellek for reading the chapter on 'The Psychology of Art'; Henri Peyre and Harold Bloom for their incisive criticism of the final manuscript. I have often benefited from W. M. Frohock's *André Malraux and the Tragic Imagination* (Stanford, 1952). For the translation of passages from Malraux's novels I have made use of current works listed in the Bibliography, but have occasionally changed them according to my understanding of the text.

I

Abiding the Question

THE famous scene with which *La Condition Humaine* opens shows a man about to kill. He mutely interrogates his victim, a sleeping figure with only one foot visible as living flesh; the rest is obscured by a mosquito net's white gauze. The killer is named Tchen; about the victim we know nothing. Malraux gives at the top of the chapter the exact date (March 1927) and even the time (half an hour past midnight) perhaps to reduce our consciousness, like that of Tchen, to a single point.

The author catches every absurd intrusion of an outside world on this island moment of thought, as the murderer tends towards his inevitable act. 'The only light came from the neighbouring building—a great rectangle of wan electric light cut by window-bars, one of which streaked the bed just below the foot as if to stress its solidity and life. Four or five klaxons screamed at once.' He also renders certain equally absurd ideas which intrude on a mind faced by the irrevocable: 'That foot lived like a sleeping animal. Was it attached to a body? "Am I going mad?" He had to see that body—see it, see that head.'

Tchen's consciousness, which is brought so near to us, cannot sever the warp of the real, the 'world of men', from the woof of the absurd and utterly strange. Whatever realism exists is at the same time an interrogation of the real. The strong illusion of immediate life, conveyed by this close-up of the mind of a murderer, is actually an artistic means to stage a metaphysical drama. Though Tchen's act may determine the success of a revolution, he is no more, as yet, than a man assaulted by

> those obstinate questionings
> Of sense and outward things,
> Fallings from us, vanishings;
> Blank misgivings of a Creature
> Moving about in worlds not realized. . . .

Malraux has often said that art is an interrogation of the world. The novel, in particular, seems to him the successor of poetical tragedy, because it confronts Man with a world he has not made, and deepens our awareness of fate by deepening Man's power to question it. In the above scene, however, it is Man himself who feels obscurely put into question. A simple query—'Should he try to raise the mosquito-netting? Or should he strike through it?'—produces in Tchen a moment of intense anguish; not because of fear, or moral scruple, or even because of the psychological difficulty of killing a person in his sleep. All these reasons are touched on but subtly discarded as Malraux goes from the surface of the anguish to its depth. Only when Tchen suddenly sticks the dagger into his own arm does the reason for his bewilderment become clear.

Tchen has suffered a loss of identity, of *human* identity. His sense of Man's presence is deprived by this oppressively inhuman atmosphere. The sense of time has already vanished in this moment which is like a question-mark, and so has the victim as a human person. The white gauze neutralizes his body: that foot is like an animal. Tchen even loses the image of the resistance of flesh in this world not of Man, and so plunges the dagger into himself. But his own blood also vanishes as a human fact. 'Tchen shuddered: an insect was running over his skin! No!—blood trickling. . . .' Then, most ghastly, the sleeper, when Tchen has entered the area of light to see him, suddenly mocks his purpose, seeming to become a corpse before his eyes: 'To touch this motionless body was as difficult as to stab a corpse, perhaps for the same reason. As if called forth by this notion of a corpse, a grating sound issued from the man's throat.'

A mere murderer might have welcomed a trance veiling the too-human in himself or in the victim. It seems (we do not yet know his political motive) that Tchen comes to perform an act springing totally out of Man's courage and redounding totally to the power of Man. Yet, as he proceeds towards the kill, he learns that his act will escape him, like his own arm or blood no longer recognized as *his*. Tchen does not find Man, but, perversely, all around him, shadow-images of that which denies Man. He sets out to find Man delivered from the gods, and in so doing discovers the gods—at least a world questioning and mocking Man's presence.

Malraux's art of interrogation cannot, at first sight, bear comparison with that of the great tragedies. In Greek drama the gods still have the power to pose questions which man cannot elude. Nothing seems more natural than that Attic cascade of queries and answers exchanged between man and man to interpret his exact measure in the face of oracle or catastrophe. Though the answer to the riddle of the sphinx, as to Greek tragedy itself, may be 'Man', in both cases the *questioners* are more than human. For Man to know his measure the Gods accuse Thebes with a plague and Oedipus with his own questions.

What accuses or questions Tchen? Nothing concrete or external, except, perhaps, an alley-cat, the shadow of whose pointed ears grows beside the bloodstain on the victim's bed. 'He jumped: miawing! . . . Its eyes riveted on him, it stalked through the window on noiseless paws.' It seems a last representative of the all-seeing gods. Tchen certainly appears more like a sleep-walker than like a man in full control of himself. From the time that he stands 'fascinated' by the white cloth of the mosquito netting to when, chasing the cat, he suddenly finds himself on the balcony before the stars and sparkling streets of Shanghai, things impinge on him so quickly that he moves less than he is moved. The fast, proleptic rhythm [1] dehumanizes the place of his action, so that Shanghai strikes Tchen as a rediscovered human land. 'He stayed and watched the stir of the cars, the passers-by running beneath him in the lighted street, as a blind man who has recovered sight looks, as a starved man eats.' It is as if he had ascended from hell; Tchen, in fact, uses the phrase *remonter chez les hommes* and describes this blank-walled room as a *lieu sans hommes*.

Thus, in a sense, Tchen questions himself by seeking the face of death, the face of what denies Man most strongly. But, testing his strength, he discovers his isolation. Pyotr Stepanovitch, in Dostoevsky's *The Possessed*, tries to bind his anarchists together through having them perform a murder. So Tchen, perhaps, wanted to bind himself to the society of Man by some irrevocable act. He finds himself only the more estranged: on leaving the hotel and hearing again a human voice, he does not know whether to hit or to embrace the speaker. 'The murderer of a life or of other more secret things [says Malraux in an early work] may discover that he is penetrated by his crime *or* by the new world which it imposes on him.' Tchen eventually accepts a new universe from which even the last divine accuser of Man, death, seems to have vanished. Or rather, Tchen seeks now to make death *his* act of accusation. Shortly after this first murder he hurls himself with a bomb at Chiang Kai-Shek's car. But the general is not in it—he has many cars.

The event again questions Man's power of self-determination. Ironically Tchen not only fails to kill Chiang, he even botches his own death. Still half-alive after the bomb has exploded, he is forced to kill himself a second time by putting a pistol directly to his mouth. Tchen's very failure, however, serves to make his accusation one against Man's fate, not against a particular idea, person or social order. And this remains true of Malraux's protagonists as a whole. Revolution offers them a possibility of arraigning the human condition. The success of the movement with which they affiliate, though important, is still a by-product. Tchen does not give a single thought to the paper for which he has been sent to kill the man in the hotel room (it authorizes a delivery of fire-arms), and almost forgets to take it after the murder. Only when, from the balcony, he hears the arsenal's siren announcing the relief of the night shift, does he recall his mission: 'Stupid workers, coming to manufacture the fire-arms destined to kill those who are fighting for them. . .!'

The workers' blindness, however, is the same fatal blindness that dogs Tchen himself. His contemptuous remark reflects the Marxist criticism of the workers' status in a Capitalistic system. Marxism would solve the contradiction of Capitalist societies, in which the workers work against themselves, by collectivizing the means of production. But can it solve that universal contradiction, basic to the world of tragedy, which makes it impossible for man to 'trammel up the consequence', and for Oedipus to foresee the end of his questions? Just as Tchen's murder plunges him farther into solitude instead of into communion with Man, so the course of events in Shanghai will make his sacrifice to the revolution work against the revolution. The arms which Tchen purchases with blood are, after the insurrection, handed over to Chiang Kai-Shek by order of Moscow, and enable him to crush the Communists with their own weapons.

Malraux shares in the quest of resurrecting tragedy without its gods. These have lost their power to confront Man with himself. What is Man? The one who must define, question and accuse himself, the one who is, as Baudelaire writes, both knife and wound, victim and executioner. Tchen twice lacerates himself before killing, the second time with the words 'The complete possession of oneself . . .' The only thing that may question man *qua* man, not merely *qua* individual, is his own act, by which he tests the soul in an extreme and wilful manner.

This suggests a comparison between Tchen and Dostoevsky's Raskolnikov in *Crime and Punishment*. Why does the latter kill the pawn-broker? He finds, after the crime, that he has no interest in her goods, and that he has known this all along. Tchen, it is true, kills for a specific political purpose. Yet we learn about it only when it again enters his mind after the murder is done. Moreover, when Tchen brings the paper to his fellow conspirators, they find that while it authorizes a delivery of fire-arms, these are not paid for in advance. In a sense the whole thing must be done again, just as Tchen, later, must kill himself twice over, or Raskolnikov, is forced to murder both the old lady and Lizaveta (only one of Dostoevsky's 'doublings'). The specific act in both cases proves to have no function except to test strength of soul; any further reason it may have—Raskolnikov's moral disgust or Tchen's politics—is a secondary consideration. Georg Lukács, who traces the development of individualism from Balzac's Rastignac and Stendhal's Julien Sorel to Dostoevsky's characters, helps to illumine this continuity between Tchen and Raskolnikov. He remarks that 'the concrete act becomes more and more a thing of chance, is the occasion rather than the real end or means. In its stead . . . the psychological and moral dialectic comes to the centre: the testing out of whether Raskolnikov really possesses the quality of soul to be a Napoleon. The concrete act turns into a psychological experiment. But one whose stake is the whole physical and moral being of the experimentor; one, moreover, whose "occasion" or "chance object" is a stranger's life.' [2]

Garine, in *The Conquerors*, and Julien Sorel, in *The Red and the Black*, both study the *Memorial* of St. Helena. The lineage of Malraux's heroes goes back to a century which called Napoleon a 'Professor of Energy' (Balzac) and Christ 'that thief of energies' (Rimbaud). Yet Raskolnikov's experiment, viewed through the art that produced Tchen, expresses less the tragedy or absurdity of the individual, of the one thrown back entirely upon himself, than that of Man, the one who acts to transcend the human condition and in so doing confirms it. The solitary act of an individual has become a sufficient fictional means to call into question the strivings of humanity as a whole—Raskolnikov, a student, and Tchen, a terrorist, not Oedipus, King of Thebes, or Macbeth.

This qualification does not touch a fundamental acuity in Marxist criticism. The abiding problem, raised by Lukács about Dostoevsky and by Sartre about Malraux,[3] is that of the characters' deeply negative sources of life. 'In the end is death'—the act is merely a reaction to that consciousness. Tchen, for example, has no being except in the face of death. Malraux has called the meditation on death, which plays so large a part in his work, a characteristic of periods in which Man feels alienated from the cosmos.

The Marxist interprets this alienation in his own way, and envisages its transcendence through a historical process transforming the negative sources of individual action into more positive social reactions, until a perfect political order is achieved. Tragedy, in this light, is a historical and purely transient expression of Man. The concept of a *modern* tragedy, therefore, must seem very close to defeatism. Yet it is clear that Malraux does not consider the individual as a tragic figure *qua* individual. He remarks in the well-known preface to *Days of Contempt* (1935):

The history of artistic sensibility in France for the past fifty years might be called the death-agony of the brotherhood of Man. Its real enemy is an unformulated individualism which existed sporadically throughout the nineteenth century and which sprang less from the will to create a man whole than from a fanatical desire to be different. . . . The individual stands in opposition to society, but he is nourished by it. And it is far less important to know what differentiates him than what nourishes him.

To create (by art or act) is always to become conscious of an inner fatality, some previously unrealized dependency by which Man is secretly sustained. Whatever Man creates also creates an inescapable consciousness of that which denies or transcends him. Tchen becomes a tragic figure when his own act questions him, not as an individual or as a murderer, but as everyman who must convert some fatality into a purely human act of will, yet is betrayed (like Macbeth) by his secret dependence on forces alien to Man.

What victory may be obtained in this world where consciousness is always that of the act alienated from the agent? Simply, perhaps, to keep acting. In Malraux's novels it is less the particular act which is problematic (should a or b or c be done? . . .) than the man himself, who harbours a deep reserve on the effectiveness of human action in general. Katov, a fellow conspirator of Tchen's, asks a native Communist leader how many of his men would know how to use fire-arms if the insurrection were to take place the following day. In thinking about the question the man's face assumes an absent-minded look. 'An intellectual, thought Katov.' He is right: the man was not thinking of an answer but of difficulties. (Do we have enough arms anyway. . . . And what's the use of arms against tanks?) The real heroism is to sustain the motive for action in the full consciousness of the apparent absurdity of action.

Malraux does not disdain psychology in creating his characters but explores a relatively new domain: the psychology of men confronted by the will to inaction in themselves or in others. Axioms flow from him or his characters as if an unexplored geometry of action were being revealed. It is not by chance that his first three novels deal with an Asia where jungle, opium and even art deck a deep-seated distrust of the efficacy of Man's act. One of his fascinating—at times annoying—mannerisms is to interrupt the narrative with sharp notations of an external world indifferent or incomprehensible to Man. A good instance is that pervasive smell of burning, whether of human flesh or materials, which emanates equally from the jungle of *The Royal Way* as from Madrid of *Man's Hope*: it also comes to Tchen just before he leaves on his suicide mission. The tragic sense, according to Malraux, is inseparable from this deep-seated, psychic enemy: 'When I say that every man feels, powerfully, the presence of fate, I mean that he feels—and almost always as a tragic thing, at least at certain moments—the world as independent of his act.'

Yet Malraux occasionally depicts a further victory over fate, linking us to that strangely triumphant feeling evoked by much greater works. The sentiment of the tragic is seen to grow out of man's victory, not over death, but over that in man which death aims at: his uniqueness. That 'eternal recurrence' which characterizes fate, and which Nietzsche accepted so forcefully, is understood and humanized. The tragic sentiment is evoked most purely not by multiplying lives (the stuff of comedies, of Winter Tales), but by repeating the chances of death, of unique, fatal acts. A hero like Tchen, or his fellow conspirators Kyo and Katov, dies more than once.

By a curious and beautiful *doubling* he is permitted to convert an act which indicates the presence of fate into one which also shows the presence of Man. The very force that frustrates human action, making it necessary for every act to be repeated, exalts the death of men who chose to repeat to die. Katov's case is, perhaps, the most poignant, for he chooses twice a lingering over a quick death. Crowded with other wounded Communists into a schoolyard near a railway station, he notices a free space and starts to move painfully towards it, not knowing that it is reserved for those who are to be tortured. Some prisoners prevent him, but a short time after this a Kuomintang officer enters, has him singled out and directed to that empty space. The accident serves to focus attention on that space, but is also, perhaps, a bitter joke suggesting that Katov secretly anticipates or even conspires with his fate.

When the inhuman whistle of a locomotive, into whose boiler the wounded Communists are thrown, sounds for the third time, two young Chinese, separate from him on his left, cry silently in terror. Katov then seems to confirm his complicity with fate, his terrible attraction to the utmost that could put man to the test. He opens his belt, containing cyanide, but instead of using the poison for himself, smuggles it to the young men—there is only enough for two. In the darkness of the compound, however, one of them drops the cyanide: a shadow of the vanity of even the supremest action. . . . While looking for it the hands of the searchers touch, then one of them seizes Katov's in a fraternal gesture, thanking him for his sacrifice whether in vain or not. The scene might have ended here. But something is found, perhaps the cyanide, and Katov to make sure demands the 'pebbles' back, recognizes their shape, and—returns them. The first giving of the cyanide could have been the work of a fatality, a temptation which possessed Katov rather than vice-versa: the repetition authenticates.

The striking thing about Malraux as artist or thinker is his refusal to separate the idea of Tragedy and the idea of Man. Many have written about the tragedy of Man without God. For Malraux, however, the tragedy of Man is not caused by the absence of something else, Man being irreducible. Yet every definition has involved the idea of his *specific difference* which is one ground for his sense of the tragic. We recall Pascal's formulation of this specific difference: 'Man is only a reed, the weakest thing in nature; but he is a thinking reed. . . . Though the universe should crush him, Man would still be nobler than his destroyer because he knows that he is dying, knows that the universe has got the better of him; the universe knows nothing of that.' Malraux's writings share the Pascalian accent, but a subtle if important reorientation of the idea of Man has intervened, often called existentialism. The specific difference is no longer conceived to be something added (over Nature) or a disproportion (above Nature, below God). It is thought to reside in Man's power to sustain his ability to act despite his burden of knowledge. The *sense* of his specific difference, that he knows what crushes him, does not define Man, but raises him to the level of tragic action. It is a certain quality of consciousness which follows a prior act, and without this act it is useless to talk of Man. The act questions the man, makes him realize inescapably—like Tchen—the existence of forces not reducible to human measure. And this shadow which falls 'Between the idea and the reality, Between the motion and the act', or which follows it, is tantamount to the consciousness of death or of the world's indifference, and makes Man's heroism possible. For though he is the one who knows he must die, who knows what crushes him, that is not his true definition.

'In the end is death' negates 'In the beginning was the act'—the hero continues to act in the face of that negation.

Tragedy has always shown Man under the shadow of an accusation he cannot entirely remove. He is questioned inescapably in the name of a greater power. That question, verging on accusation, which goes from Job to God, has first gone from God and the Accuser to Job, and ends as a justification of whatever in Man can abide it: 'Gird up thy loins now like a man, I will demand of thee, and declare thou unto me.' God is the eternal scourge of men, remarks a critic-friend of Malraux's, whether they are intent upon creating or destroying him.[4] But if the divine loses its power to accuse, if the very idea of God is no longer understood, what tragedy—and what nobility—are possible?

The difficulty of resurrecting tragedy without its gods, of making Man his own accuser, becomes concrete as we glance at the tragico-comic transformations of a Dostoevsky character. Raskolnikov is Man in search of a divine inquisitor, though forced to question and accuse himself. But Kafka's K: accused by everything and by nothing; Eliot's Prufrock: the man who no longer dares to face the question; Tchen: the man whom only death can question; Camus' Stranger—who can question him, or the inhabitants of Oran, self-blinded to the plague of the gods?[5]

Haunted by the dynamism of the West, Malraux will identify Man with his act, even though this act is vain and leads only to the greater awareness of death. Yet this awareness is the divine accuser who keeps Man permanently in the realm of the tragic. *La Tentation de l'Occident*, his first mature work, shows how this identification of Man with his act and his act with death is the source of the historical greatness of an Occidental civilization born of Greece, 'with harsh Minerva face, with her arms, and also the stigmata of its future madness'.

II

The Sickness unto Action

The best lack all conviction, while the
worst
Are full of passionate intensity.

Yeats

La Tentation de l'Occident, reportedly begun in
1921, was not finished till 1925, when Malraux
had already seen political action in Indo-China
and perhaps Canton. It purports to be an exchange of letters between Ling, a Chinese student
in Europe, and A.D., a Frenchman in China, both
displaying the sensibility of a Claudel and the
fearless analytic verve of a Valéry. The form of
the book is somewhat deceptive, since the clash
of Eastern and Western points of view results in
the recognition of Man's unity and a defence of
the West as the tormented bearer of that belief.
Where Ling sees the West as a single culture kept
alive by an absurd flaw, A.D. recognizes in its
torments Man's universal dilemma brought to
full consciousness.

Ling puts first things first and begins with an
analysis of love. The European appears to use it
as a dynamic instrument to destroy conventional
concepts of reality. His deepest wish is to sacrifice, and to have the beloved sacrifice, whatever is

25

considered most 'real'—religion, judgment, morality. Instead of building up the established order love serves to alienate him from it, and such a wilful game of *désagrégation* is utterly strange to the Oriental, who, far from exploiting love's disorder, seeks in all things a careful extinction of the ego-passions, 'une attentive inculture du moi'.

Ling develops this difference into a radical distinction between the two cultures. The Oriental always judges himself from a cosmic point of view as a fragment of an immeasurably larger and more vital sphere; the European measures all things by man, by the duration and intensity of a single human life. Since this measuring stick, in the face of the cosmos, is hasty and perishable, the European must continually engender new myths, new concepts of reality that remake the world in the image of Man. His behaviour in love reflects his awareness of the superficial nature of all these concepts. Their outmoding or transformation, moreover, is now so rapid that the Western mind finds itself seriously divided between the equally intense claims of many possible myths. Nietzsche said that 'God is dead', but Ling goes beyond and behind that statement when he claims that 'Man is dead': his mythmaking powers are failing to produce any adequate, unified world-picture.

It is clear that Ling challenges by his analysis two ideas which Malraux persists in defending to the present day. The first is the idea of Man itself, the other that of his unity. Ling questions the latter by his assumption that West and East are radically different cultures, and the former by showing that the West, because of its insistence on Man as the measure of all things, has fallen prey to an increasingly self-destructive dynamism. In his answers A.D. accepts Ling's picture of the West but not his interpretation of it. He rejects the idea that the difference in culture correctly described by Ling argues a difference in the human condition of French and Chinese. The landscapes of East and West reveal the same defeat of man, the same tragedy. The Chinese waste, evoked at the beginning of the book, has swallowed up all its conquerors; while Europe, in the closing pages, is apostrophized as a 'vast cemetery where only dead conquerors sleep'. The only difference between the two civilizations is the desire of the East not to forge an idea of the specific difference of Man, and this is as arbitrary and self-defeating as the more positive, mythical systems that keep the West restlessly alive.

The profoundest parts of this book are those in which Malraux, like Pascal in the *Pensées*, faces the spectre of Pyrrhonism, the idea that fate has so overwhelming a dominion in this world that even Man's victories ironically hasten his defeat. A.D. clearly harbours as deep a scepticism of Man's power *vis-à-vis* the world as his Oriental counterpart. He admits that actions never achieve their end. The Greek notion of Man as the measure of all things first encourages the act, yet in Greek tragedy the act betrays this very notion of Man. Some knowledge of such a betrayal underlies all of Western sensibility, moved more by the will to power of great personalities than by their actual success. What did St. Helena matter or that Julien Sorel ended on the scaffold! And the crisis of modern Europe is, according to A.D., simply the realization that Western activism still ends in a cemetery of dead conquerors.

How can the European admit this defeat without abandoning, like Ling and his culture, the very idea of Man? Instead of equating fate with the cosmos and its ultimate harmony, he equates it with Man and his unquiet transformation of any given order. Everything with the power to accuse, scourge or deny Man, everything called Fate or God, is really internal to one who conspires against himself, being his own dynamo, his own best enemy. 'After the death of the sphinx,' we read in the *Tentation*, 'Oedipus turns against himself.' The only thing that, from this perspective, can defeat Man is the idea of Man itself—an idea *into* which Malraux's heroes die.

La Tentation de l'Occident throws many interesting lights on Malraux as novelist. The bloodiness, violence and torture which he evokes are clearly extreme interrogations (not less real for being fictional) which Man inflicts on himself to sustain the idea of Man. Whatever the apparent cause, it is still he who puts himself on the wrack. The search for the accuser, death, is a dominant theme. 'In order to destroy God, and having destroyed him,' writes Malraux, 'the European mind annihilated everything which could stand in opposition to Man: the goal of its efforts attained . . . Man finds nothing but death.' Thus the search for death remains an extreme form of Man's search for himself. In a highly significant essay, 'D'Une Jeunesse Européenne', published a year after *La Tentation*, Malraux states his thesis less cryptically:

> Sorrow of a tenacious Occident in search of its unity! The old unrest which made men torture themselves and weep tears of horror at their own image; which led them to be butchered, weeping, before the Christian God or to fight him to the point of madness—today raises itself up against its only remaining object: Man. A conflict begins between the deepest forces of Being and this almost unseizable object *which cannot be vanquished*.[6]

The self-castigations of Man reflect his quest for self-definition, for unity—a quest finding systematic critique in Camus' *The Rebel*. The evolution of the novel of adventure (Malraux's included) seems to confirm this view of human history as a tormented search for the realization of the idea of Man. Robinson Crusoe, for example, is only indirectly concerned with the idea of Man: it is Nature, reluctant to yield her treasure, which opposes and haunts him. With Ahab, in Melville's *Moby Dick*, the motive for the search becomes more complex, and the idea of treasure takes second place. The main characteristic of the white whale is that it obsesses Ahab, that through it he hunts himself. The plot, in its purest form, is related to that of the self-pursuer, who tracks down his own crime or terrible origins. It fuses the detective or adventure story with ancient tragedy to give the formula of the modern novel: *Cherchez l'Homme*.

Malraux's novels show that the more Man becomes conscious of his mystery, the more he tempts this consciousness and faces death. A typically Western yet intrinsically human sickness unto action ensues, which cannot be overcome without abandoning the idea of Man for an Oriental kind of quietism. The temptation of the West is to extend the realm of Man's self-consciousness despite the danger it involves to his survival: of Ahab's crew only Ishmael survives. Thus Malraux shares the crisis of humanism which overtook the European intellect between the two wars. Valéry's famous essay on 'The Crisis of the European Mind', Thomas Mann's entire work, Spengler's *Decline of the West*, Eliot's *The Waste Land* and Buber's *What is Man?* point to the same storm-centre. Some of these writers move with humanism to transcend it; Malraux moves within humanism to reconstruct it. He shows man seeking action and death to survive them with increasing vigour.

III

In Search of Man

WHAT is remarkable about Malraux's major novels is not only that they seize, as Trotsky has remarked, the modern theme of revolution, but also that they seize it on the wing, at short remove. *The Conquerors* (1928) deals with a strike against British interests at Canton in 1925, *Man's Fate* (1933) with the Shanghai insurrection of 1927, and *Man's Hope* (1937) with the beginning of the Civil War in Spain. The last-mentioned novel, therefore, is practically battle-field reportage. The speed of fictional interpretation illustrates a first principle of psychological warfare: controlling the impact of an event as close to its occurrence as possible. Malraux's own swiftness in seizing on the event does not, however, indicate his will to constrain it to any simple meaning. His art aspires to a preventative insulation of events—events in danger of being annexed by the fast-moving propaganda of a deterministic view of history.

The appeal to history (instead of to reason or authority) in the struggle to tell right from wrong, requires an ever-ready, journalistic speed of interpretation. The power to make or remake public opinion becomes as important as the facts themselves, which are always complex, incomplete or neutral enough to permit several meanings. Faced with History as the ultimate court of appeal, the artist has two choices. He may resolutely avoid contemporary or historical fiction, faithful to the old precept that political events should not, except in disguised form, become the subject of art, until invested by time itself with aesthetic distance. Or, knowing that nothing will be left neutral but is digested at once by political machines, and not wishing to renounce his own immediate influence on men's minds, he may try to beat the propagandist at his own game, not so much by showing the shallowness of any immediate annexation of historical events as by emphasizing the deeply tragic, humorous or ironic discrepancy between Man's energies and their historical result. Malraux chooses the latter way: he finds a non-political ideology to immediately interpret contemporary events, an ideology which seeks to be specifically and exclusively that of an artist.

The speed which Malraux displays in giving fictional form to political events reappears as part of the fundamental rhythm of his earliest novel, *The Conquerors*, and yields a clue to the *a priori*, artistic nature of his point of view. Not only does the plot, because of the theme of revolution, move inherently fast, but Malraux chooses a narrative technique that augments the impression of haste. The story of the strike is told by means of an unnamed first-person narrator who uses the present tense throughout and treats us to a dazzling on-the-spot commentary sprinkled with asterisks, apothegms and question marks. An additional heightening of urgency comes from the fact that he is still a fortnight from Canton when the strike begins. In the first part of the novel, 'The Approaches', he impatiently pieces together bits of knowledge about the strike and about Garine, the hero of the book.

Garine is in charge of intelligence and propaganda at Canton, and has transformed a comic-opera organization into a powerful agency. Although Borodin, a representative of the Communist International, is nominally the head of the strike, it is Garine on whom attention centres and who plays the critical role. The narrator has not seen him for a long time, and all the information he can get, as he voyages towards Canton, only increases Garine's mystery. We feel, as the narrator sifts rumour after rumour, the dilemma of a mind always at some distance from the central event, and therefore always outdistanced by or running after it. The dilemma of the narrator is comparable to that of Garine, who, at Canton, is the target of innumerable demands following upon another as precipitously as messengers at certain points in Shakespeare. Garine, like the narrator, wants to know or control a series of things always running beyond personal knowledge and control.

This repetition in the story of a haste inherent in its narrative form suggests that *The Conquerors* is about a universal human condition rather than about a specific political event. This is borne out by a plot which moves from 'The Approaches' (part I) through 'The Powers' (part II) to 'The Man' (part III), and from clear external dangers to more subtle, internal ones. In fact, the nearer Garine comes to victory the greater the threat of internal enemies, as if the removal of outer and political dangers revealed the abiding presence of an inward, universally human tragedy.

This tragedy is related to the fact that we cannot tell, at the end of the book, whether Garine is conqueror or conquered. As lamps are often darkened, in the exotic landscape of Malraux's novel, by insects attracted to them, so all things revolve around the single person of Garine and yet, finally, destroy him. Take Garine away— the revolution fades into a muddled, insubstantial pageant, into the primitive swarming passivity or reckless energy of China. Yet what is the hero, ultimately, amid this Frankensteinean revolt? China, says one of the principal characters, has always conquered her conquerors. Though everything depends on Garine till the very last minute (when he saves an army from being poisoned), he continually calls into being forces beyond his control. A sample of Malraux's prose will indicate this:

'Several banks? Good. Let them attack.'
He hangs up and goes out of the room.
'I follow you?'
'Yes,' he calls from the passage-way.
We go down. The men with armbands, whom Nicolaëff has just selected, come up from the cellar bringing rifles, which their

comrades on the doorstep are distributing to the unemployed, almost in rank; but the coolies from the coast station have been bringing up boxes of cartridges; the armed men mingle with the others, who are pushing forward and trying to get cartridges before they have been given rifles. Garine shouts in broken Chinese; no one listens to him. So he comes forward and sits on an open cartridge case. The distribution stops. There is a pause. What is happening? is being asked in the rear. He makes the unarmed men fall back, has those with rifles placed before them. The latter, in groups of three, and with exasperating deliberation, pass by the cartridge cases and receive their ammunition. In the cellar the coolies open new cases with hefty strokes of hammer and screw driver. Outside the sound of distant marching as before. We can see nothing through the crowd. Garine leaps on the steps and looks:

'The cadets!'

Yes, here are the cadets led by Klein. Coolies are coming up from the cellar, panting beneath the new loads of cartridge cases hanging from bamboo poles and crushing their shoulders. Klein stands before us.

Malraux's first-person narrator is clearly more than a journalistic device. He provides a fixed point against which speed of action is measured (' "I follow you?" "Yes" he calls from the passage-way'). Not so much speed of physical displacement as that of events relative to *personal* consciousness. The author's technique doubles the tension between viewing the person (Garine + Narrator) as focus or master of events, and viewing these events as uncontrollable. The final effect, however, is that as the hero 'leaps' towards the event, the event itself 'leaps' towards him, and makes him a mere catalyst. The hero hastens his doom: the faster, the more efficient his acts, the quicker his obsolescence. In the course of the story Garine acts again and again for a cause which finally rejects him with the sounds of the Red Army approaching Canton—'metallic . . . punctuated by the rhythmic fall of hammers'. It will deny the very thing which saved it, his 'bourgeois malady' of individualism. Its sounds are the sounds of fate as well as of Communist discipline.

There is, in fact, a basic similarity of plot between Malraux's major political novels. They show or prefigure the triumph of a cause together with the death or disabling of the men chiefly responsible for it. The scheme is clearest in *The Conquerors*, least evident in the complex panorama of *Man's Hope*. Yet the plot is at work even when, as in *Man's Hope*, the novel precedes the end of the conflict and so anticipates history. The anticipation helps to explain the author's ability to translate at short remove decisive political events into fiction. He believes in a conception of Man which history cannot affect and whose truth depends on this fact. Henry James said of Balzac's accumulation of realistic detail that he wound reality around him like a boa constrictor. So Malraux, in a similar combat of strength, winds living history around him to sustain his idea of Man.

He identifies (*vide* Chapter I) tragedy with Man and not with history, which remains a sequence of revolutions, changing into oppressive forms, and inciting new upheaval. Man is not *Man* unless thrown back upon himself, and not *tragic* unless he accepts to act again despite the knowledge of his return to nakedness. A successful rather than abortive revolution (as in *The Conquerors*) only emphasizes this tragedy in the context of an apparent historical triumph. Man's tragedy is more than his defeat, but it is also more than his victory.

Thus Malraux broaches the question of whether a man can conspire with historical forces. His tragic hero is a type of Faust who incites the spirit of Revolution, and finds that this demon, like all of his kind, serves Man only at a price—the death of the humanistic ideal, of the respect for and reliance on individual lives. Garine seeks a power to action which transcends that of the single person, which is truly national or fraternal in scope, and might even achieve that triumphant march of 'humanity', the subject of Victor Hugo's and Michelet's historical epics. What is Garine really? A creator, like Balzac's Vautrin, or like Napoleon in Julien Sorel's imagination. He creates by—propaganda; yet, as he remarks, one cannot always choose one's means of strength. He is the alienated intellectual, forced to find his sphere of influence outside his own country. Born in England he might have been an arch-colonialist. 'Empire is—one tenacious, constant act of violence. To direct, to determine, to constrain. That is life.' But the demon who helps him in this endeavour wears an inhuman or anonymous face. Garine's own face, at the end of the novel, is so hollowed, that it seems to be his death-mask: in a highly symbolic act he peruses it with a pocket mirror as if no longer sure of its identity.

It is tempting to pass directly to *Man's Fate*; yet *La Voie Royale* (The Royal Way), published in 1930, has considerable power as an experiment, and shows the author adapting thriller and adventure story to his dominant conceptions. The formula *Cherchez l'Homme*, foreshadowed by *The Conquerors*' basic movement from 'The Approaches' to 'The Man', and from political to deeply internal forms of menace, will enter literally into part of the novel's plot. Otherwise the situation remains that of Malraux's previous novel. We find a young adventurer (Claude Vannec) whose thought is filled both with a great project and with an older man (Perken). Instead of a strike or revolution to rouse a people from centuries of torpor there is a plan to rescue the art treasures of deserted temples along Indo-China's Royal Way. The Asiatic jungle-world that conceals these treasures, and threatens the innermost will to action of Claude and Perken, is clearly a symbolic counterpart to the China that threatened those other 'conquerors':

Some unknown power assimilated the trees with the fungoid growths upon them ... Here what act of Man had any meaning, what human will but spent its persistence? Here everything frayed out, grew flabby and soft, tended to assimilate itself with its surroundings, which, loathsome yet fascinating as a cretin's eyes, worked on the nerves with the same obscene power of attraction as the spiders hanging there between the branches, from which at first it had cost Claude such effort to avert his gaze.

The will of the adventurers is sustained, in the first part of the novel, by the thought of hidden treasure—although the 'treasure' means very different things for the two men. But when the art works are found, and Perken and Claude, deserted by most of their helpers, must pass through the territory of savage tribes, only the thought of another *man* secretly in control of this jungle-universe keeps their spirit alive. This man is Grabot, a fellow adventurer of Perken's, who has disappeared into this region. Grabot is to Perken's imagination what Perken is to Claude: the mystery man who has absolutely no ground for living, no gods, no hopes, nothing but primordial courage. Emerson defined the hero as the immovably centred person, and Grabot is immovably self-centred, indistinguishably *vir* and *virtus*, ruthlessly denying his dependence. Feeling repulsed at the sight of a scorpion, he deliberately gets himself bitten. 'Once a man decides to cut himself off completely . . . from his fellow men,' says Perken, and it applies to him as much as to Grabot, 'he's always bound to inflict terrible sufferings on himself, simply to prove his strength.'

Instead of this Grabot of legend, the adventurers find a slave, blinded and tethered to the grindstone by the savages, unrecognizably human, turning round and round to a tinkling bell. Questioned as to what happened, Grabot utters one word: 'Nothing.' The lesson is clear. Claude, Perken and Grabot are impelled to confront and solve the riddle of the sphinx, the riddle of a universe which denies the *idea* of Man. To each this denial appears in a personal way: what the 'otherness' of Woman is to Perken, dead temples and artifacts are to Claude. The jungle through which they pass denies Man's permanent place at the apex of Creation. That 'silence of the infinite spaces' which gripped Pascal is recreated by savages staring 'with blank inhuman fixity; their eyes . . . dead and stony, facets of the universal silence.' The adventurer cannot accept the answer: *nothing*; his life is bound up with making the sphinx answer: *Man*—so the believer would force *God* from all created things. Despite Grabot's 'nothing', Perken cuts him loose and walks cataleptically towards the savages, hoping to destroy that answer in his own flesh. His courage wins the day, but he dies later before Claude's eyes, wanting to make even death 'his' act, dying nevertheless in an absurd and lingering fashion.

The Royal Way interests mainly as an anthropological allegory. In order to paint the image of a new kind of man it projects a new kind of world. But, in a sense, this very power of projection turns out to be the subject. We are shown a world in which Man deprives himself of his ordinary environment, of all given values, so as to gain a new, more totally human and self-posited milieu. The question, What is Man? can no longer be answered except by determining the nature of the world he imposes on the world, the type of relationship adventurers (or novelists) substitute for a given one. Cut off from the usual channels of communication, from marital, political and and social relationships, all the characters of this book seek 'Grabot', Man utterly free from the absurd compromises imposed by fate. Yet Grabot, pared down to sheer courage, ends in total blindness, going round and round the treadmill of compulsion. He becomes, even more than Garine, the slave of the forces he has sought to master, and his aspect, when Claude and Perken see him, is no longer human. Malraux's conception of Grabot does not add very much (except a certain expressionistic simplification) to Kurtz of *The Heart of Darkness*. But while Conrad's power as a novelist is superior, Malraux possesses the characteristically French gift of the philosophic or dramatic parable also found in Sartre and Camus. Grabot, as a type, incarnates the mystery about which Nietzsche speaks: 'Was it not necessary to sacrifice even God, and, out of cruelty to oneself, to worship stone, stupidity,

gravity, fate, nothingness? To sacrifice God for
nothingness—this paradoxical mystery of the
ultimate cruelty has been reserved for the rising
generation. . . .'

Malraux entitles his next and greatest novel *La
Condition Humaine*. Political in subject, it is, like
The Conquerors, more than political in range, and
deepens the definition of Man explored in the
previous books. Of the novel's seven chapters,
the first two tell of the quick success of the
Shangai insurrection, while the remainder portray an ironical, protracted series of events, re-
ducing the characters one by one to solitude. Because, in the first part of the story, they can still
impose their world on the world, they also succeed in imposing their will. Yet, from the outset,
a contrary pattern prevails, ripened by apparently external circumstances. Soon every character suffers an experience of self-estrangement
through which he becomes aware of the radical
gap between the world and his view of it. A
moment of 'the silence of the infinite spaces'
mocks his deepest dreams, and, though it may
not alter his will to act, suggests a contradiction,
inescapable in its nature, between Man and
History.

In this book Malraux's architectonic vigour
surpasses any shown before; it almost convinces
us that the form of the novel is the natural
medium for his view of life. The premise that
Man inevitably imposes his world on the world,
that thought and act are fictional in essence,

grants the slightest event the same expressive potential as the greatest. It is true, at least, that Malraux's power of *development* has advanced. We can take, as an example, his treatment of what was probably the germinal incident of the novel. Towards the end of the *Psychology of Art* he remarks:

Every man's self is a tissue of fantastic dreams. I have written elsewhere of the man who fails to recognize his own voice on the gramophone . . . and because our throat alone transmits to us our inner voice I named the book *La Condition Humaine*. In art the other voices do but ensure the transmission of this inner voice. The artist's message owes its force to the fact that it arises from the heart of silence, from a devastating loneliness that conjures up the universe so as to impose on it a human accent.*

The incident to which the author refers occupies an unobtrusive section at the beginning of the novel. Kyo is listening to records prepared by the conspirators, which purport to teach a foreign language but actually transmit secret messages. Kyo, who does not recognize his own voice in recorded form, thinks the disks have been changed or that the phonograph distorts, but the matter is quickly dropped. Malraux allows the event to interpret itself by haunting the consciousness of Kyo, who associates more and more persons with it. When, for example,

* Translated by Stuart Gilbert, published by Pantheon Books, New York, 1949.

he tells his father (Gisors) about the estranged voice, the latter explains: 'We hear the voices of others with our ears, our own voice with our throat.' And he adds, astonishingly: 'Opium is also a world we do not hear with our ears.' Thus one germinal detail gathers momentum and begins to symbolize the human condition in its entirety. Gisors himself takes opium, and it seems that every man, wittingly or unwittingly, finds a way to overcome an irreducible solitude. The world of Man's perceptions is, like that of the artist, a second birth, a world conjured up to impose on it a specifically human accent.

As with the detail so with the persons. There are many characters now, none really minor, and all affected in various ways by a radical experience of estrangement. Kyo fails to recognize *his* voice; Tchen did not recognize *his* arm. Some, like Gisors, are always aware of an inner desolation; others, like Kyo, the man of action, who distrusts his father's tendency to convert every experience to knowledge, only by usurpation or chance. The death which overcomes Malraux's heroes is no more than the symbol of an ultimate self-estrangement. And even those who survive do not always escape it.[7]

Malraux is, at last, in full possession of his idea. He has found a law encompassing all 'fatality', and can give each of his characters an individual and widely varying fate because they are still instances of that law. Man, as *The Royal Way* had implied, is defined by the world he imposes on the world, not potentially but actually. Man's fate, the present novel adds, follows from his nature. What is *fate* except an inextricable involvement with the world, one which comes about because of the nature of Man, who wants to make the world inseparable from his life?

That this attempt, however vital, must fail, is the *condition humaine* out of which Man's greatness and tragedy spring. Malraux stands close to the existentialistic thesis that we 'invent' our fate in order to be irremediably bound to the world. But even though every such 'invention' reveals a specific power in Man to impose his world on the world, it is also an escape from his intrinsic solitude, and leaves an anguish that tells he is greater than the sum of his acts.

The multiplication of individual destinies is also part of a more relaxed and 'epical' narrative manner. Tchen still runs to his fate as if action were a drug against solitude which wears off and had to be increased. But others move at different speeds, and reach their fulfilment at different points in the plot, which is no longer in a state of continuous high tension. The specifically *literary* problem which Malraux solves in the present novel is how to convey Man's pursuit of fate without the artificial, fantastic tempo of *The Conquerors* or the conglomeration of synthetically staged adventures we find in *The Royal Way*. His problem is of the same order as that of an artist who strives to obtain a three-dimensional effect with two-dimensional means, to show that the medium does not have to be of the same nature as the thing it represents. All problems of this order are essentially aesthetic and imply that artistic freedom consists in the power to represent an experience without being subject to its law.

If we compare two incidents, of how man runs towards his fate, one from *La Condition Humaine* and the other from *The Conquerors*, Malraux's new artistic freedom will appear in greater relief. In the latter, Klein, a friend of Garine's and fellow-worker in the strike, is taken hostage by the terrorists and killed. Garine and the narrator are told that a number of bodies have been found and go to identify them. As a morbid joke the terrorists have propped the bodies upright, and for once the narrator's speed of perception fails: 'As soon as I raise my eyes I see the four bodies, *standing*.' The author here suggests two things: an event too quick for human eyes, and that Klein's body *is* death, as if death had been within him as a hidden fatality. The slashes on Klein's face, perceived later, express a further trick of fate: Klein was always terrified at the idea of knife-killings. Then Garine wants to close his comrade's eyes, and, with a blindly foreseeing gesture, puts two fingers 'stretched apart like scissors' on the white eyeballs—realizes the murderers have cut the eyelids off.

The scene described above is one of the finest in *The Conquerors*. It haunts the mind by its compression and its obsessive emphasis on the faculty of sight. It seeks to show that fate is quicker than Man, and yet within Man, who anticipates and even conspires with its action. A very different scene, expressing the same idea, occurs just before

46

Kyo listens to his voice and does not recognize it. Very casual, it is enlivened by a single naïve gesture. Tchen has just informed his comrades of the completed murder, and feels a great need to leave them and confide in Gisors, because no one else, except perhaps Katov, is really close to him:

The Russian [Katov] was eating little sugar candies, one by one without taking his eyes off Tchen who suddenly understood the meaning of gluttony. Now that he had killed he had the right to crave anything he wished. The right. Even if it were childish. He held out his square hand. Katov thought he wanted to leave and shook it. Tchen got up. It was just as well: he had nothing more to do here; Kyo was informed, it was up to him to act. As for himself, he knew what he wanted to do now. He reached the door, returned however.

'Pass me the candy.'

Katov gave him the bag. He wanted to divide the contents: no paper. He filled his cupped hand, chewed with his whole mouth, and went out.

'Shouldn't 've gone 'lone,' said Katov.

A refugee in Switzerland from 1905 to 1912, date of his clandestine return to Russia, he spoke French almost without accent, but he swallowed certain of his vowels, as though to compensate for the necessity of articulating carefully when he spoke Chinese. Almost directly under the lamp, very little light fell on his face. Kyo preferred this: the expression of

47

ironic ingenuousness which the small eyes and especially the upturned nose (a sly sparrow, said Hemmelrich) gave to Katov's face, struck him all the more as it jarred with his own features and often troubled him.

'Let's get it over with,' said Kyo. 'You have the records, Lou?'

The passage effects a transition from one personal focus to another, from Tchen to Kyo. In so doing it swiftly illuminates the relationship between both and the third main character, Katov. Though the latter is a pivot he appears mementarily in greatest relief: his personality is an *unknown* which Tchen and Kyo (and Hemmelrich) cannot solve. Katov is often kept opaque, and he does not hold the centre until the last great scene of his sacrifice and death. Still, we are often shown into his thoughts, and if he remains mysterious here it is because Malraux always chooses some opaque pivot around which actions or thoughts turn. In Tchen's first scene it is the victim shrouded by the white gauze; in Katov's last scene the strangely empty space of the prison compound; and often such an obscure experience as that which Tchen wishes to clarify with Gisor's help, or that which Kyo puzzles over after hearing his voice in recorded form.

Malraux's characters are defined by their different reaction to this 'unknown'. All are drawn towards it like Perken to the idea of torture, or Claude to his map, or the conquerors to

'China'. But now Malraux varies more skilfully the structure of each fascination, its momentum, form and quality. Both Tchen and Kyo subtly transform the other man, make him less strange, more at one with their wishes. The manner in which each imposes his world on the world is, however, quite different.

Tchen is strongly conscious of his solitude, his increased familiarity with death, and wants to deny it. He thinks he understands Katov's 'gluttony', but when the latter misinterprets his outstretched hand, we are reminded of the distance between any gesture and its interpretation, as well as of the distance between Katov and Tchen which the latter would have liked to deny. Yet Tchen accepts Katov's misunderstanding too quickly, and his returning for the candy, and gulping all of it, has something equally hasty about it, this time wilful rather than spontaneous. [8] It may reflect the speed with which he moves towards his 'fate'. As for Kyo, he tends to pass over differences in character, proceeding by the quickest route to the next item: 'Let's get it over with . . .' He too, therefore, displays a certain haste. Katov, finally, appears kind and relaxed, but there is the suggestion of gluttony and that curious 'swallowing of vowels'. The whole scene has a great deal of humorous strength not found in any of Malraux's previous work except his fantasies. [9]

The estrangements of which we have talked always occur in the midst of the secret haste the above passage hints at. When the records are played, Kyo hears a voice he does not recognize as his own. Despite the fraternal effort of revolution, all the characters, by the end of the novel, come to face death or destiny alone, strangers to themselves and to the world. The moment of death is, in fact, associated with this leit-motif of the strange voice. Just before Kyo joins Katov in the prisoner compound and takes poison, he passes through an experience in which it plays a deeply disguised role.

König, Chiang Kai-Shek's police chief, in charge of rooting out the Communist revolutionaries, has heard that Kyo is a believer in the 'dignity of Man'. He therefore has Kyo brought from prison and plans to make him betray his belief. During their interview the telephone rings and a voice asks whether Kyo is *still* alive. Soon it rings a second time with, apparently, the same query. König, in the meantime, has begun an aimless interrogation. Does Kyo want to live? Is Kyo a Communist through . . . dignity? Kyo, who does not see a purpose to these questions, tensely expects the telephone: when it rings a third time König lets it ring, hand on receiver, asking where the Communists have hidden their arms—another pointless question, since he already knows the answer or does not need Kyo for it. Then, suddenly, Kyo understands that the telephone is merely a piece of stage-business.

What business Malraux does not say, but König is obviously not interested in specific information. He wants merely the gesture of betrayal, and later offers Kyo his freedom in exchange for it. The business of the telephone, a devilish variant on the game of one two three . . . gone, is rigged up to achieve this end. For the repeated ring suggests more than a limit to Kyo's life which König (the name perhaps symbolic) has the power to suspend. It evokes the *indifference* of the world—that repetitive machine, that strange anonymous voice—to Man's existence and will. The real temptation faced by Kyo is not König's power or his humane offer but the subtler suggestion of this voice. It demands nothing except the sacrifice of an idea, the idea of Man. The inhuman whistle of the locomotive which later pierces the prisoner compound, the scene of Kyo's and Katov's death, is the image of König's telephone raised to the height of impotent terror.

The tragedy Malraux depicts, and which the world of *Man's Fate* embodies most clearly, does not stem from any special flaw in the protagonists. It comes, at first sight, from the brutal confrontation of Man with external fate. Yet each of the novels shows a reversal in which external forms of fate appear as invited or even invented by Man. A later work such as *Man's Hope*, in which the author feels even freer towards his idea, suggests this reversal also in occasional images, as when Loyalist aeroplanes appear to *seek* the enemy's anti-aircraft fire. Malraux's view should, however, be distinguished from religious and psychological concepts of fate. The former may hold that a person creates what he deserves, the latter that he creates for himself what he most deeply wants or is compelled to want because of early experiences. For Malraux there is a fatality prior to every individual fate, and this lies in the specific nature of Man, who cannot accept a world independent of his act, and so aspires to identify himself with forces greater than his being, even at the risk of losing part of his humanity. This risk is expressed in the general theme of self-estrangement, as well as by the symbols of alienated or inhuman face and voice. König with his telephone and the atrocious whistle of the locomotive has donned the mask of fate: he is assimilated to what has crushed him and propagates its horror compulsively. But the tragic, rather than demonic, figures show their greatest strength as they stand alone, betrayed by the forces they have called up, deeply conscious of their power not to be seduced. Katov and Kyo wear their own faces and speak with their own voice.

IV

The Return from Hell

Wer spricht von Siegen? Überstehen ist alles.

Rilke

Malraux's development, after *Man's Fate*, is illumined by a comment of his on Dostoevsky, Cervantes and Defoe, writers separated as much in spirit as in nationality, whom he joins nevertheless in a surprising collocation. 'All three,' he remarks in the year of his next novel, *Le Temps du Mépris* (1935), 'wrote of the counterpart of solitude, the reconquest of the world by a man who has returned from hell.' The remark has a direct bearing on all his novels, but especially on the sequence beginning with *Le Temps du Mépris*. This novel (whose title is best translated *Days of Contempt*) tells the story of a militant Communist named Kassner who survives solitary confinement in a Nazi prison and returns home deeply marked by the experience. It is the first work in which the author depicts the survival of the hero as well as of his cause, and so departs from the purer tragic structure which exacted the death or disabling of a major character. The hero's 'descent into hell' is now accompanied by a 'return' to the world of men, a return susceptible of various interpretations but increasing in thematic importance.

For Malraux's earlier heroes there was no return. Their actions led simultaneously to self-awareness and self-estrangement. They paid every step towards consciousness with a step towards utter solitude, so that the fullness of the knowledge of man corresponded to the fullness of solitude, or death. Katov and Kyo do not become as gods, knowing good and evil, but as men, knowing death. The return of the hero means, in this light, an emancipation of the knowledge of Man from that of death or solitude. He attains a vision of mankind without suffering an irremediable experience of isolation.

Although the theme of the return is absent from Malraux's first novels, it is still deeply implicit in their form: they contain an Ishmael, a character who survives and whose function is to tell what he has witnessed. In both *The Conquerors* and *The Royal Way* we have such a witness, a younger man who watches an older man (the hero) die. The author, strictly speaking, does not need such a figure, since the convention of the novel gives the role of witness to him. What Malraux seems to represent through the separate person of the witness is a possible separation of the paths leading simultaneously to the knowledge of man and to death.

While the figure of the sustained first- or third-person witness disappears in *Man's Fate*, a new and important development is found which we have mentioned in another context.[10] The style itself intimates the author's freedom from the law to which his world remains subject, so that if the idea of Man remains inseparable from the idea of tragedy, the idea of the artist pairs with the idea of freedom. To discover the meaning of style, says Malraux in reference to Goya, is to understand that 'the way to express the unusual, the terrible, the inhuman, is not to represent carefully an actual or imaginary spectacle but to invent a script capable of representing these things without being forced to submit to their elements'. The implications of this concept are not worked out in their complexity until we come to *The Psychology of Art*, and even there are more eloquent than clear.

Man's Fate is also the first book explicitly to raise the question of the survivor. Malraux, instead of ending with the deaths of Kyo and Katov, adds a moving epilogue in which May, Kyo's wife, and Gisors, his father, argue about the function of the surviving revolutionary. What 'return' to the world is possible for him? The answer of both is deeply wrong in so far as neither really proposes his return to the world of ordinary, peaceful action, but rather a calm rejection of life (Gisors) or a vengeful remembrance of the dead (May). The figure of the survivor remains ambivalent: we do not know whether he can return to daily life or whether his sense for it has been mortally injured.

In *Days of Contempt* the question of the survivor moves from epilogue to centre. The plot of the story shows a dream-like repetition of the hero's first descent into 'hell', the Nazi prison in which Kassner was confined. It possesses a power analagous to the subversive climate of China, the clandestine violence of the Cambodian jungle, and Tchen's white-walled room in which Man loses his sense of identity:

> Only a sly, submissive kind of sub-human creature grown utterly indifferent to time could adapt itself to the stone. Prison-Time, that black spider, swayed back and forth in their cells as horrible and fascinating as the Time of their comrades sentenced to death. . . . Something in him attempted to adapt itself, yet adaptation was, precisely, stupor. . . .

The prison does not threaten Kassner with clear, external forms of danger. It plunges him into the thought that he is irremediably separated from the world of men. The fear of being buried while conscious rouses in him the temptation to forget his identity as a man, to adapt himself to whatever frees him from consciousness. This *fascination du néant*, as Malraux calls it in a later novel, is man's deepest and most secret danger. The prison's literal purpose is to soften Kassner for interrogation by cutting his links with the outside world; its symbolic purpose to erase from him the very idea of Man.

This place where Man is estranged from himself is the scene of the most arduous *Cherchez l'Homme* ever described by Malraux. Kassner invokes every human memory in his possession against his crushing solitude. Where all imaginative defences fail, a fellow prisoner's tapped code establishes a moment of real human communication and saves him from being decisively cut off—he is drawn back into the world of men and composes an imaginary speech to members of the party until his release. This occurs when an unknown person surrenders under his name, taking his place as he had taken that of a comrade.

Though Kassner survives he remains deeply unsure of his identity. The problem of identity plays, in fact, a crucial role in the entire plot. Kassner is saved from death when the Nazis cannot identify him. Later he is saved from prison by the unknown person taking his name. A pilot risks his life to fly him to Prague without knowing anything about him except that he is a party-member. At Prague, finally, Kassner has the futile experience of wishing to locate his wife among a crowd of a thousand similar faces at a mass demonstration. Thus his life, when he comes up from hell, is simply an oblique repetition of that adventure. Even in the world of men he must continue to search for Man.

He succeeds in his search; but the more each experience strengthens a fraternal vision of man, the more it puts his personal identity in doubt. Kassner remains a shadow not a person; an interchangeable part not a unique existence; back home he must remind himself that his wife is alive, and she is afraid to be alive, knowing he will leave on other missions. The absence of descriptive detail, as well as the stripped nature of the plot, in which some have seen Malraux's poverty of imagination and others his power to create types, reflect Kassner's ambiguous position midway between *everyman* and what Heidegger calls *das man*.

His return is not, therefore, without its price. That curiously strict scheme of compensation which, in the previous novels, demanded the death of the hero in exchange for his full understanding of the idea of Man persists in slightly modified form. Kassner's solitude is overcome only with a distinct loss in personal identity. The picture of an endless chain of substitution arises as one Communist sacrifices himself for the other. Kassner is delivered by 'Kassner'. Malraux already approached this view in depicting the Narrator–Garine, Claude–Perken type of relationship: the younger man absorbs the experience of the older and becomes, potentially, his redemptive double. If fate imposes anonymity, Man aspires to synonymity.

Hence man's freedom is no more than to substitute one man for another, or one fatality for another. An ironical sequence, common to all the novels, reaches every level of the plot. All of the hero's attempts to escape the grip of fate are still re-presentations of it, and this applies as much to his experience after returning to the upper world as to his sufferings in the underworld.[11] There is no victory once for all—a fact inscribed even on Kassner's hand, which is said to bear two life-lines. One was made by himself, ironically, with a razor, the other 'had been made not with the stroke of a razor but with patient and steadfast will; what was man's freedom but the awareness and organization of his fatalities?'

In *L'Espoir* (1937) both concepts of Man's power (that of the razor-line and that of patient organization) are proved insufficient. The book describes the attempt of the Spanish Republicans to transform their raw, idealistic fervour into a force capable of fighting Franco, who commands an army much superior in discipline and equipment. The novel may be divided into two main parts, which correspond roughly to Malraux's own (I, *Illusion Lyrique*, II, *Les Manzanares*), although the construction is symphonic rather than linear, so that motifs cross and intermingle in both parts. 'Descent' and 'Return' are not apparently separate movements as in *Days of Contempt*, but their lineaments remain.

The first part shows the heroic insufficiency of men who follow a razor-straight line and sacrifice themselves without the possibility of return. The ideal of the noble warrior, who conquers by exemplary gestures in the nineteenth-century revolutionary tradition, is purged in blood and defeat. People like Puig, the Anarchist, or Captain Hernandez, an army officer of the old school, die voluntarily and too quickly, sacrificed to their particular idea of the revolution rather than to its success. The most ironic example of their inutility comes when Mercery, a French *miles gloriosus*, dies in a grotesquely heroic moment dousing Fascist aeroplanes with a water-hose.[12]

In the second part survival and victory, not heroism, are the main theme. 'Our humble task,' says Garcia, the Loyalist's chief of Intelligence, 'is to *organize* the apocalypse.' During the process of organization, the Communists, well trained in obedience, and faithful to party rather than to individual, inevitably replace the Anarchists as the core of Republican resistance. The turning-point of the war comes when Manuel, the only 'pure' Communist among the central characters of the book, halts the rout of the Republicans, and refashions them by using a Communist cadre. But it is also Manuel who, estranged from his men through the responsibilities of command, understands in the very moment of victory the price it exacts: 'Every day I get to be less human. . . .'

Malraux, however, adds a postlude entitled 'Hope'. In it he augments a tension that exists between the external signs of victory and the inner consciousness of the victors. The latter understand, as in Malraux's first novel, that Man is always both conqueror and conquered. In so far as he fights against others he also fights against himself, as if every life that is lost were a subtraction from the life of Man as a whole. The hope in his heroes which secretly goes *beyond* victory is that the triumph of one power will not mean the death of some other. Manuel, in the final pages of the novel, goes off to listen to Beethoven and to dream of the infinite possibilities in Man's life

—not, perhaps, the most orthodox Communist meditation. With excited voices proclaiming the statistics of victory ('Kilometre 93! . . . 94! . . . 95! . . .') he thinks of something far removed from Kassner's razor-straight line. The sounds besieging him transcend, by their very diversity, the immediate, bloodfilled and monotonously intoned present.

The artist's entire skill pits itself against what may be called the razor-concept of human destiny, but within a world which demands it, and is justified in its demand by the artist himself. It is hard to imagine a greater tension. Malraux would respect the single-minded will to action, yet portray the tragic dualism of agent and act which springs from it, and preserve (at least in his own artist consciousness) what Garcia calls 'corpses', alternate voices and destinies rejected by the present. The result is a sustained structural counterpoint—so sustained, in fact, that *Man's Hope* is often as 'paralysed' as any novel of Flaubert's. That ultra-human speed first expressed in *The Conquerors* resolves more curiously than ever into an ironic intervention of new obstacles or into the simultaneous presence of all powers, the moment of truth in which Manuel discovers the unpredictable possibilities of life, the moment of art and fairyland 'in which those who are killed all come back to life'. It is not a matter of chance that the world of art intrudes as theme and source of vision into many pages, because art alone stands beyond victory and defeat, preserving to human consciousness whatever is

61

swept aside by the sharp decisions of the immediate historical present.

The most obvious way in which Malraux modifies the idea of an absolute victory is by his continual use of the *trompe l'œil* and 'double-take'. An occasional device in previous novels, it now assumes the proportions of a method and serves to express the eye's effort to achieve straight-line interpretations. But just as actions, in Malraux's world, must constantly be doubled or reaffirmed, so must this movement of the mind's eye. In one scene, for example, Manuel watches his tanks advance, and as he looks, their line assumes the form of a crescent so that they seem to be turning back—he realizes they belong to the enemy. A liaison car pulls up with an officer in it relaxed and snoring—what Manuel hears is a death-rattle. He can't see the officer's wound because it is in the back of his neck, *presumably* this one had turned. Manuel then takes his field-glasses and sees men running towards the Fascist tanks, which apparently do not fire, for no one falls. He refocuses his glasses—his men are going over to the enemy. While wondering why another of his companies is moving forward to certain death ('Couldn't their captain recognize Italian tanks?') this captain is carried up dead, a bullet in his back. Manuel realizes at last that these facts together spell internal treachery.

The movement from an external to an internal form of menace is also characteristic, and repeats a sequence first found in *The Conquerors*. For

Malraux's novels are, fundamentally, about civil war: Spanish against Spanish, Chinese against Chinese, man against himself. If so, it is absurd to think that Man can conquer himself without defeating himself, so that the dilemma of Western activism appears once again lighted by a glaring contradiction. *L'Espoir* inherits yet another device from *The Conquerors*, the 'obstacle-course' plot in which things happen so quickly that as soon as one danger is overcome another like it stands in the way. So many inimical facts bombard reader and victim that suspense dies and the concept of victory is again put in doubt. A good example is Sembrano's experience. When bullets riddle his aeroplane, he asks the second pilot to catch hold of the controls, but the latter is grievously wounded. He then decides to use his weakened arm, but his arm has 'disappeared' . . . After the aeroplane crashes, one of the crew reaches a telephone—the wires are cut; another finds a truck for the wounded—no gasoline; they drain off the aeroplane's gas—the truck's magneto has been sabotaged. . . . Thus Malraux's warriors always face a monster who will sprout two more for every head cut off.

All these inventions project external as internal danger, fatality as will, or the finite act as an infinite repetition. They may be grouped under the general term of 'prolepsis', a well-known figure of thought which reverses temporal or spatial perspectives. An especially fine instance occurs when Hernandez watches the Fascist firing squad which will soon come to him:

They leap perilously backward. The squad fires, but they are already in the ditch. How can they hope to get away? The prisoners laugh nervously.

They won't have to get away. The prisoners have seen the leap first, but the squad fired before that. Nerves.

Nothing 'beats' death: the apparent movement to evade one's fate is really its consummation. Malraux's irony does not have the prisoners or Hernandez as its target but a *metaphysical haste* which characterizes man in the face of the world, and of which the physiological reflex is a basic sign. The scene of Hernandez' execution is a fine extension of this irony, for the methodical shooting of the prisoners, three by three in a hot, pervasive atmosphere, evokes sentiments not of death but eternity.

Malraux, like Valéry in *Le Cimitière Marin*, questions that 'holy impatience' which is inseparable from Man. The counterpoint structure of his novel establishes a rhythm very similar to Zeno's arrow, which vibrates, wings on, yet never moves. We have studied, in the main, features of style which are manneristic, but these point to a technique shaping the whole. Malraux perfects his usage of short narrative units which he juxtaposes neatly and elliptically by cinema methods of 'fade-out' and 'montage'. Through this art of antitheses he finds for every fact a further fact that questions, compensates or opposes it, and again disturbs the notion of an absolute victory. The descent of the aviators, for example, the novel's most moving episode, and one in which the author uses repeated views of a procession winding slowly down a mountain, comes after the apocalypse of fraternity has been 'organized', yet shows in the peasants, in the wounded and through the over-arching consciousness of Magnin a spontaneous fraternal passion which is ageless and beyond organization. Or when two airmen (Leclerc and Attignes) have successfully bombed a gasworks, causing a tremendous explosion of red-and-blue flame, they suddenly notice that their aeroplane, flying between two layers of cloud sealing them from the ground and the moon, glows with a ghastly blue phosphorescence: 'The measure of all human gestures was lost: far from the instrument panel, the only visible light in the waste of air around them, that sense of well-being which follows on all combat was disappearing into this geological tranquillity, into the mystic union of moonlight and pale metal gleaming as precious stones have gleamed for countless ages on the extinct stars.' The counterpoint of gaslight and moonlight, of human success and a moment of inhuman beauty that mocks it, is far too mechanical. But it shows Malraux intent on finding ironic doubles that throw completed acts against a timeless field.

In *Man's Hope* Malraux has achieved a novel which depicts the necessity and vanity of action by the same stylistic means. The idea of victory is put in doubt: every conquest demands its sacrifice, and the survival of man, as the return of the hero in the previous novel, depends on actions that involve a deep loss to his humanity. The idea of Man, however, is not put in doubt. It survives through the consciousness of the artist, that is to say of his surrogates, figures like Garcia, Manuel and Magnin. It is they who, in victory or defeat, revive what Coleridge called 'the dread watchtower of man's absolute self'. They see exactly what is gained and what is lost, yet do not despair at the manichean nature of action. *Man's Hope* realizes a symbol aimed for but never achieved in *Days of Contempt*. There the journey downward, into hell or utter solitude, remains a separate movement from the return of the hero to the world of men. The *descent* of the wounded aviators, however, seen against 'the deep gorges into which they now were plunging, as if into the bowels of the earth', and through the artist-consciousness of Magnin, is not a descent into hell but a triumphant communal return to life.

In *The Walnut Trees of Altenburg* [13] we start, for the first time, with the fact of survival. The narrator is a prisoner of war who tells the story in his own person from Chartres Cathedral, converted by the Germans into a temporary prison camp. Not only is the novel (with the hero removed from the sphere of immediate action) reflective in structure and mood, but the Cathedral's permanence at once overshadows it.[13a] Vincent Berger, the hero, is a reincarnation of Magnin watching the wounded men and offering glimpses of their individual yet similar destinies, though all are now part of, or associated with, one family, the Bergers. He describes a sequence of descents into solitude, each accompanied by a return to the world of men, except that the grandfather of the family commits suicide shortly after his son's home-coming—a relic of the stricter pattern of substitution we find in the preceding novels. The narrator, a Berger of the third generation, is already at several removes from that strange and mysterious death, of which he learns through notes left by his father. It is with these, entitled 'My Encounters with Man', that he compares his life and fashions the substance of his story.

The experiences of Berger *père* and *fils* are strikingly similar, a 'prefiguration' mentioned by the narrator himself. Events replace and repeat one another as in *Days of Contempt* and suggest an eternal recurrence with subtle progressions. The important fact characterizing the life of all three Bergers is that they are solitaries. But the form of their solitude, and their means to overcome it, vary significantly. The grandfather, angry with the Catholic Church, remains within the community, worshipping Christ from the ground outside the Church building. The father is a T. E. Lawrence type of adventurer, who supports the Young Turk movement even in preference to his own national obligations. In the First World War, Alsace being a part of Germany, he participates in a poison-gas attack against the Russians, and later joins his soldiers, horrified at the inhumanity—'Man was not created to moulder' says one of them—in rescuing the victims. In the Second World War, Alsace once more a part of France, Vincent fights against the Germans—a fact which once again shows the essentially civil and internecine nature of war. But now neither solitude nor fraternal action can be shaped into forms of protest as in the case of his fathers. In the half-blind tank which carries Berger to the front, the tank-crews are as isolated from each other as from their enemy. The only communication between Vincent (the guide) and Prado (the driver) is a piece of string which breaks at the critical point. The soldiers in that tank do not live in a world of men. War is no longer, even among fellow soldiers, a fraternal effort, but reduces all participants alike to an inhuman solitude.

A return of the Same, as if fated, seems to govern the lives of grandfather, father and son. 'I am anxious to come to the point where writing, at last! will no longer be a mere change of hells,' says Vincent, prefacing the last adventure he depicts. This episode, in which he and his companions fall into a tank-trap, expect immediate death, then return to the world of men, is as fearful as the gas attack witnessed by his father. Both reveal a demonic parody of Man's power to impose his world on the world. The touch of the gas translates everything at once into a living death ('The form of the flowers was almost intact. Just what corpses are to the living . . .'), which is also the nature of the ground over which Berger's tank is rolling:

> Of the ancient accord between man and the earth nothing remains: these fields of wheat over which we roll and pitch in the darkness are no longer wheatfields but camouflage: it exists no more, this earth of harvests, there exists only an earth of traps, an earth of mines. . . .

There has been an irreversible advance beyond the grandfather's sphere of influence, which was one small community in France. The very earth itself seems now to depend on Man's power for good or for evil: he can make it assume either the form of his affliction or that of his love. The concern of the writer is not for one region or religion or even for the larger-scale conflict of various nations: it is the survival of Man on earth. The enemy of Man, for Garine, Perken and others, was 'Asia'. The enemy of Man for Möllberg, principal speaker at the Altenburg colloquium, who has spent his life preparing a truly Germanic book on 'Civilization as Conquest and Destiny', is 'Africa'—the terrible African wasteland before which the idea of Man pales and over which his manuscript lies scattered. But the enemy of Man for Vincent Berger is Man himself, not fate, gods or earth.

This crisis is reflected in the very nature of Malraux' art. He has said that the writer defends himself against his obsession 'not by expressing it, but by expressing something else with it, by bringing it back into the universe'. This 're-petition-compulsion', however, still relieves suffering by a transference of suffering, and does not draw man out of the vicious circle that defines him as the form of his affliction. It involves more and more of the universe until today Man's fate and that of the world are barely separable. Man conspires against himself in Malraux's novels because he *is* the world. The novelist's structural repetitions integrate an obsessive anguish into the world, yet each recurrence shows more intensely how treacherous is this identity of human and universal. 'It seems,' says Berger, 'as if the tank were crawling of its own will toward a snare dug by itself, and as if the human species were beginning, this very night, their struggle with each other, beyond the human adventure. . . .'

Despite this crisis, the novel looks more firmly towards survival than any of the others. Here, where Berger replaces Berger, and the synonymity to which Man aspires in *Days of Contempt* is a natural rather than artificial thing, each alienation from the world of men results in the hero returning with a greater degree of consciousness. For the grandfather, as for Malraux's earliest heroes, there is no return: the fullness of his knowledge is also the moment of his death. Just before he takes his own life, he remarks that if he had another life he would choose to repeat his own. This strangely Nietzschean comment shows that his suicide is not an act of despair. The father experiences several moments of alienation and return, which give rise to many pages of reflections, not to one cryptic dictum. But the consciousness nearest to and yet most removed from death is that of Vincent, the artist. It can pass through hell without taking hell's form or that of forgetfulness. After escaping the deadly earth of traps and mines, Vincent looks at the land around him with innocent, fraternal eyes: 'It seems to me suddenly as if man came from the depths of time only to invent a watering can.' Behind these words is a feeling, rare in the work of Malraux, for a life in accord with nature, a deep respect for the slow, generative powers of an earth which has always outlasted man's self-destructive haste. But when Vincent adds, at the end of the novel, 'I know now what those ancient myths mean which tell of people snatched from the dead,' he expresses Malraux's belief that the idea of Man is more dependent on the evidence of the artist than on the evidence of history.

The first-person narrator of *The Conquerors* attempts to catch up with history by running after it as quickly as possible. The author parodies or transforms techniques of realistic narrative so that the journalist becomes an artist despite himself, and we are given, finally, an *ecce homo* rather than the history of a revolt. But the narrator of *The Walnut Trees* knows from the start that Man is his concern. The enemy, for him, is not an external menace, this or that nation, this or that historical event. After the fall of France, in the absence of clear and present danger, he still rescues from the void of his prison images of Man's resistance to the void. Explicitly an artist ('To write is here the only means of continuing to live'), he expresses Malraux's maturest thesis, that the idea of Man is involved with the power of art to remind us of it.

V

The Psychology of Art

THE three-volume work published in 1947–49
as the *Psychology of Art* was actually planned before the war and destroyed in manuscript by the
Nazis. Since the war Malraux has devoted his
literary activities almost exclusively to writing on
the visual arts and editing fine photographic reproductions of Goya, Da Vinci, Vermeer and
world-sculpture.[14] *Les Noyers de l'Altenburg*, published in 1943, remains his last work of fiction.

Every artist, said Baudelaire, becomes necessarily, fatally, a critic. But not so necessarily a
critic of media different from his own. Malraux's book-reviews and prefaces, though of
interest, cannot rival his dedicated concentration
on painting and sculpture. The reason may be a
matter of deeply personal preference linked to his
first love—archaeology. The cryptographer's
instinct for the secret code, the hieratic sign, the
mutilated statue and the hidden greatness has always surpassed in him the more sensuous charms
of the perfect or the self-enclosed: his apprecia-
tion of the sensuous element is, in fact, always
subordinate to his understanding of art as a
sign. Perhaps the plastic arts, having a more
difficult history of transmission than literature, because more tightly linked to the ritual

surrounding death, possessed a greater intellectual attraction.

Yet European and especially French writers have been traditionally men of letters rather than connoisseurs of one genre. The names of Voltaire, Diderot, Baudelaire and Valéry come immediately to mind. Malraux has remarked amusingly on the difference between America and Europe in this respect. In the United States the love of ideas and a wide culture are, according to him, the prerogative of college professors. American novelists, on the other hand, remind him of European painters—'the same apparent indifference towards almost everything except the desk and the bottle. . . .' But this great proportion, in Europe, of writers who seek to cross national boundaries, and for whom the visual arts are one way of so doing, is in itself significant. Europe, whether or not a political fact, has always involved the idea of cultural universality.

At the end of the First World War Malraux was 17, and the idea of Europe as the guardian of universal values had suffered its greatest shock. The end of the war also saw the publication of Spengler's *Decline of the West*, which denied (like Möllberg in *Les Noyers*) the continuity of civilizations, seeing each as a separate organism that traverses a cycle of barbaric birth and overcivilized death. Spengler's view of history threatened the whole notion of Man's unity, and hence the value of Western culture as a heritage regained and handed on by every generation. If the soul of each culture dies with it, there is no chance of the present understanding the past, no more than a butterfly the world of a caterpillar.

Emmanuel Berl reported in *La Culture en péril* that Malraux talked of the necessity of refuting Spengler as early as 1928, and there is evidence that *La Tentation de l'Occident* (1926) already seeks to reverse Spengler's thesis by using some of his own data. It implicitly denies, for example, the existence of a European or Faustian 'culture-soul', arguing that Europe is the forerunner of a world-wide humanistic culture. The influence of the Barbaric arts, and the multiplication of artistic experiments, which Spengler interprets as the efforts of a dying civilization to revitalize itself, are seen by Malraux as a unique attempt to overcome the very idea of culture as a self-contained, mortal system of values. The West's discovery is that all things, including the most diverse cultures, find their unity in Man and in him alone, so that the modern artist becomes the explorer of an infinite universe. He sets out to make the 'world with all its present and all its past, its heaped offerings of forms, living and dead', into the heritage of every single person.

In *The Psychology of Art* Malraux shows how this universal ingathering of culture is implicit in the very notion of art, and how modern painting has brought it to full consciousness. He notes, first, the changed relation of viewer to things viewed, or of artist to previous works of art. The modern museum, pitting all styles against one another, is a symbol of this change, and the magical museum of photographic reproductions (a 'museum without walls') possibly its fullest expression. That process of 'intellectualization', which began when the idea of the art gallery allowed a comparison of originals with one another, is carried infinitely farther through the invention of a printing-press for the plastic arts. As long as works of art were still experienced in place, and as long as the artist himself thought to create sacred figures, it was impossible to get to know more than a handful of masterpieces, and often in the same tradition. A Romanesque crucifix, when made, was not considered chiefly as a work of sculpture or Duccio's Madonna as a picture. But through the modern museum every vision becomes a picture and every god a statue comparable with other pictures and statues, and we learn that art has spoken a single language whatever its provenance. Malraux seems to argue that the physical autonomy of works of art has revealed in addition their metaphysical autonomy. Our grouping together of all styles has emphasized art's 'very old will to create an autonomous world'.

Malraux also notes that the Impressionists, who reduced that will to itself, did not devalue previous, especially sacred styles, but resuscitated a forgotten pantheon of religious masterpieces. The movement in art and in interpretation which begins around 1860, although intrinsically agnostic, revives the significance of *all* hieratic forms and begins a work of salvage culminating in our modern 'museum without walls'. We are, says Malraux, the first truly agnostic culture,

76

which knows it does not know the meaning of Man, but also the first to understand that every genuine work of art is linked to a world beyond the world of appearances. The *Psychology of Art* and the (incomplete) *Metamorphose des Dieux* marshall a tremendous variety of statues and paintings towards the view that history's many twilights of the divine have revealed a new absolute: art's affirmation of a world beyond the world of appearances. All cathedrals have led to the cathedral of the modern museum. But what survives in this museum is neither the gods nor the specific souls of past cultures. It is the power of Man—his power to call the world of appearances and even the creator of that world into question.

Thus Malraux, the first important practitioner of the journalistic novel, becomes one of the first popularizers of the view of art as an *anti-mimesis*. Plato held that the artist copied the copy of the Idea: his chair would always be two removes from the world of Truth which contained the chair's original. Malraux holds that the artist rebels against the existing scheme of things, considering it a spurious copy of the original. His thesis comes close to a belief recurrent in the history of ideas: that the creator of this world is not the true God.[15]

In any view of art as an anti-mimesis the concept of style becomes central. Art is defined by Malraux as 'that whereby forms are transmuted into style'. Every artistic 'rapture' is also a definite 'rupture', first with some admired model

77

of reality but finally with the whole principle of mimesis. The artist begins with pastiche and ends with style, with a schema that is more than a way of seeing, because he has abandoned representation as the end of art. 'The style of the great religious arts,' writes Malraux, 'was not merely a way of looking at the world but a systematic transposition of mundane things onto a supermundane plane.' This may be true of religious art, yet what of Athenian sculpture, Renaissance painting or Impressionism? Malraux goes on to say: 'We are beginning to wonder if the function of style in other types of art (though differing in obvious respects) be not of a similar nature.'

He faces here a problem crucial to all theories of art. It is not enough to say that 'of course' art differs from life. Does this difference have one nature, many natures? Malraux is content to show this difference as something positive and similar in both the religious and the profane styles. Modern art, though agnostic, also aspires to translate *this* into *another* world, although this 'other' is no longer a sacred world but simply a world-of-art. Just as Byzantine painters wrested the human face from the domain of the real and made it a sacred index, so modern art wrests the various sacred styles from the reality of particular cults and uses them for their purely painterly values: 'By delivering art from cultural preconceptions, the purely pictorial style enjoined today has exhumed, through half the world, forms ranging over three thousand years.'

It is interesting to see Malraux apply his concept of style to a specific case, the development, for example, of Greek sculpture. Fifth-century statues of Demeter or Athene are not, according to him, idealized portraits of young women which express the sculptor's anthropomorphic point of view. No one would recognize Athena in the most beautiful woman of Athens: to be a goddess she must first be a statue. The sculptor clearly separates his goddesses of gold and ivory, his bronze athletes, his polychrome Korés from the realm of appearance. His sole purpose is to seize the divine, and he uses the human form for this because beauty is essentially divine, incidentally human.

In Hellenistic art the statue loses its link to the divine and becomes merely statue, a means to emulate rather than break the world of appearances. Athene is, at last, an idealized woman, and the more complete the illusion the better. 'Appearance is now promoted to be the respectful judge of divine images dispossessed of the divine, as it will come to be the disdainful judge of sacred images dispossessed of the sacrosanct' [a reference to the *beau idéal* and post-Renaissance disdain for the Gothic]. Roman sculpture, finally, falls into complete illusionism and Malraux denies it the name of art.

For the first time appearance is equated with reality. That is why, though there are many artists in the Roman world, there is no Roman art in the sense that there is Egyptian,

Medieval, Chinese or Mexican art. The object of Roman art is no longer to destroy but to embellish appearance. Deified emperors are translated into Olympian style as rigorously as Byzantine saints later on into icons. The gods adorn the gardens.' [16]

Art is thus considered tantamount to a style which breaks with the world of appearances in a significant manner. This breaking-away must, however, be part of the artist's will to transform the world, a will inseparable from his nature. The artist, a Faustian, refuses every inheritance which is not a conquest. He is born into a style which he tries to assimilate, not so much for its own sake as because it frees him from the seductive and hypnotic realm of appearance. The depiction of living forms begins less with Man's response to a living model, with sensuous delight, than by his grip on the model: with the expressive sign. Having liberated himself from the world by a received system of such signs, the artist continues to free himself until he finds his own. 'The tectonic system in Cézanne's landscapes is not in conflict with the trees but with museum art.' But what has happened, in this perspective, to the world of living forms? It seems to be no more than the first mover in a chain of independent reactions.

It is strange that the first comprehensive work to acknowledge the autonomy of the visual arts should make us 'appreciate' much more than relive the original artistic experience. One often senses, in Malraux's 'history', that same intellectual or metaphysical haste which his novels also express in various ways. The press of analogies, of groupings, of pictorial juxtapositions, is so great that the works of art referred to become *illustrations* to the invincible march of the author's intellect. The value and charm of previous histories of art (and also, to some extent, of literature) consisted in their restoring the isolated work to its historical or geographical site, precisely because the general reader would have no access to this, and needed help to overcome obstacles to the direct experience of the work. Such reconstructions did not mean to substitute for, but rather to enhance, a certain kind of direct experience: it was assumed that a work of art could not be fully understood except *in situ*, just as a building stands in significant relation to its natural surroundings or any part of a cathedral to the whole.

Modern photography, however, turns all 'dependent' objects into 'free' works of art, linking them to those whose context is irrevocably destroyed by time. Hence a new and interesting problem arises: is there a context common to all artifacts *as such*? Even the charm of relics or of the most abstract works of modern art does not reside in their being without context, but in their putting the very idea of context in question. A modern painting or statue often needs no more than good light, space and a neutral background: the most that scholarship can do is to understand that simplicity and to maintain the work in it. The power in art which modern processes of abstraction have revealed seems to be inseparable from the nature of the means which have revealed it: photographs rob the artifact of its context, and that reveals a power of abstraction (Malraux would say 'interrogation') which has always defined Man—the one who can impose his world on the world, who is not in function of any particular context but the very giver or changer of context.

When we say that art or criticism is extremely 'intellectual', we mean that it does not place an object in its natural context but tries to show it as self-contained or evoking its own kind of wholeness.[17] The world, instead of being a text illumined by the work of art, becomes a pretext for a new and autonomous world, that stands to the old as a substitute rather than as an intensification ('Cézanne, Renoir and Van Gogh . . . rejected more than mere social order; they repudiated passionately and conjointly the "soul" men read into the visible world'). But the discovery that art may substitute for a certain kind of direct experience must also work against experiencing art directly. It becomes one language among many, a code to be 'cracked', rather than an absolute act of communication which sought and still seeks to shape men's lives. Referring to the rapid turn-over of styles characteristic of contemporary art, Malraux's spokesman had remarked, in *La Tentation de l'Occident*:

These works, and the pleasure they bring, can be 'learnt' like a foreign language . . . The particular pleasure of discovering unknown arts ceases with their discovery and is not changed into love.

What Malraux does make us experience more clearly than other critics is a world-of-art which he posits and which stands in the same relation to the world of appearances as Hegel's 'being or immediacy that does not have mediation outside it, but is this mediation itself.'[18] Each addition to the company of masterpieces illumines further a world-of-art common to all. In so far as art has a history, this in the nature of an infinite chemical experiment to isolate the power of autonomous creation implicit in all genius. The artist, as he becomes more conscious of this power, disengages his creative impulse from direct dependence on the antagonisms of world and time to seek it as more genuine and imperishable in the antagonisms of art to art.

An important section of Malraux's work deals with the artist's growing consciousness of his autonomy. Leonardo is said to have perfected a picture-space illusionism by means of which painters could, at last, make any subject, real or imaginary, 'come alive'. What Leonardo had really discovered was the autonomy of pictorial style, but in the period following him painters used his technique mainly for historical, mythical and religious anecdotes. By the nineteenth century the concept of the *beau idéal* ('that a picture possessed beauty when what it depicted, had it become real, would have been a thing of beauty') exercised a reactionary influence on both the theory and the practise of art.

The revaluation of the Gothic and the discovery of other 'primitive' arts freed painting of its dependence upon a subject-matter conceived in terms of the 'beau idéal'. How could Romanesque sculpture, for instance, with its hieratically distorted forms, be imagined as 'coming alive'? These ancient arts, deprived by history and museum of direct religious significance, seemed to suggest not a sacred world created and chastised by God, but an autonomous world created by the style of an artist subjecting all things to his genius instead of to Beauty or Nature. 'It now became apparent that forms of human self-expression existed which owed nothing to imitation. . . .' The picture-space of Renaissance art, which rivalled that of the world of appearance by using the latter's own means of fascination, becomes one style among many, all of which proclaim the artist's power to suggest imaginary worlds rivalling God, devil or demi-urge.

Modern art clarifies the artist's autonomy still further. It becomes purely interrogative, i.e. it specifically purges itself of all means of fascination derived from the realm of appearance and only sponsors forms that challenge the recognizable, everyday world. Malraux also notes a preference for two-dimensional, anti-baroque, and even anti-humanistic effects. According to Spengler, the Faustian culture-soul, now in decline, was marked by a 'passion for the third dimension'. Malraux agrees that the exotic arts which have been revived, and the painters promoted from lesser to greater rank (Piero della Francesca, El Greco, Georges de la Tour, Vermeer), use sweeping simplifications and dispassionate, though not unexpressive, gestures. But he draws from this a positive rather than fatalistic idea: modern art seeks to achieve a painterly medium purified of all external ends, of all charms belonging to the object rather than to the painting.

Malraux's understanding of the importance of the medium in contemporary art is one of his finest and least disputable contributions. He shows that painting, in striving to be no more than a pictorial and autotelic style, often attains a *classicism* which has remained one of the persistent aspirations of Western art. Primitive art proved to the modern painter 'that the most poignant way of expressing an emotion is not necessarily the portrayal of the victim of that emotion; that a work embodying anguish need not show us a weeping woman, and that style is in itself a mode of expression'. This comes close to Eliot's emphasis on the medium rather than on emotion and personality, and replaces the realist definition of art, 'the world seen through a temperament'; with 'a temperament seen through the world-of-art'.

It is because modern art has looked at the world as if it existed only to become a painting that it has also had the power to resuscitate so many ignored or buried styles. As soon as paintings are conceived to belong to a world-of-art rather than to particular cults they no longer stand in irreconcilable cultural opposition to one another. The most important characteristic of modern art is that it suggests a universal civilization not based on the death or negation of previous cultures.

It is clear that the question of our civilization has been raised, [writes Malraux, still thinking, perhaps, of Spengler] but it seems obvious to me that to look upon it the way we look upon all vanished cultures (Egyptian or Roman, for example) is not altogether acceptable. Because there is a fundamental difference between our culture and all the cultures which have preceded it: for us these cultures exist whereas for them each one was the negation of the one preceding it.[19]

The civilization that Malraux foresees on the basis of modern art makes no attempt to deny or appropriate history: it is content to annex every work that arraigns the world of appearance and of destiny. The 'classicism' of Cézanne unifies East and West because great art has always mastered a profound awareness of fate by a lucid horror of seduction.[20]

One feels that Malraux's conception of art is strengthened by many literary sources. One is Greek tragedy, in which the spirit of interrogation was closely linked to a deep awareness of fate. Another is Baudelaire, whose lucid horror of seduction was once taken for its embellishment, and whose classicism is the other side of his deep sense of the irremediable. But the *Psy-*

chology of Art reflects, beyond these, the psychology of Malraux's own novels: the struggle, in them, for a consciousness to survive the evidence of death, history and haunting solitude. 'Every work of art that imparts a sense of aesthetic quality links up the netherworld that it expresses with the world of day; and every work that moves us thus testifies to the triumphant element in man.'

There are important similarities between the views held by Malraux and those fundamental to contemporary theories of literature. Both minimize the historical conditioning of the work of art without minimizing history. Even Erich Auerbach's *Mimesis* is not irreconcilable with Malraux's 'Antimimesis'. The latter's interpretations would be unthinkable without that vast increase in historical knowledge which has occurred over the last hundred years. Malraux's pages abound with data though not with dates. Only the absence, in certain parts, of chronology or chronological order is remarkable; yet he admits in *La Metamorphose des Dieux* that, though his purpose there is not a history of art, 'the very nature of artistic creation often forces me to follow history step by step'. The relation between History and History of Art is curiously like that of Marvell's lovers, who will never meet though their love is parallel and infinite, and behind this view there lurks once more the tragic concept of Man. Malraux's protagonists attempt to 'make' history (the basic fiction of our age because history is the basic fatalism), yet Man's creative power, greater than both victory and defeat, cannot be identified with the historical event.

The parallel yet separate position of Man *vis-à-vis* history comes into aesthetics as an antinomy between the formal and the existential meaning of the work of art. Mimetic (existential) theories depict the artist in search of a style, antimimetic (formalistic) theories a style in search of its artist.

> The poet [writes Malraux] is haunted by a voice with which words must be harmonized; the novelist is so strongly ruled by certain initial conceptions that they sometimes completely change his story; the sculptor and the painter try to adapt lines, masses and colours to a structural (or destructive) preconception that fully reveals itself only in their subsequent work. . . . One character is replaced by another, just as, in a painting, a window too bright for the wall surrounding it, is replaced by a pipe-rack.

This view has, however, a weakness analogous to that of existential theories: it puts the artist's dependence on a non-temporal (metaphysical) scheme in the place of his dependence on history. The autonomy of art may be assured in this way, but that of the artist is once more put in question. Malraux insists against history that 'the biography of an artist is his biography as artist, that of his capacity to transform the world of appearance'. Yet he must also insist, against any metaphysical theory of inspiration, that art is a personal achievement, a personal metamorphosis of the past: 'Michelangelo, believing he was reproducing antiquity, was actually producing Michelangelo.'

The idea, common to both Eliot and Malraux, that great works of art compose a simultaneous order criticized and clarified by each new masterpiece, strives towards a solution of the antinomy. It supposes the personal regeneration of a virtually non-historical series. But it also shows how the effort to define the autonomy of the *artist* results only in a conception of the autonomy of *art*, an autonomy whose existential interpretation remains moot. Matthew Arnold, it is true, said that 'culture seeks to do away with classes', and perhaps Malraux's 'world-wide art culture' could be interpreted to envisage an ideal society of this kind. Yet, according to Malraux, the artist cannot appeal in any direct way for political changes without endangering his autonomy. He may appeal only 'to those who are, more or less, of his own kind, and, in fact, their number is increasing'. All men are potentially artists—art does not seek a perfect political structure but first the perfect man. Malraux might agree with Rilke and most of the Romantic poets that 'as soon as the artist . . . *lives* what now he merely *dreams*, Man will degenerate and gradually die out. The artist is eternity protruding into time'. But although his ultimate focus is on the artist rather than on art, he does not succeed in formulating the autonomy of the artist any more than that of Man except in terms of a world separate yet parallel to history.

Malraux's dedication to art is, in reality, a very special kind of politics called forth by the failure of humanistic philosophies to produce politically effective men of action. His aim is to reconstruct faith in humanism by sponsoring a new concept —a new myth perhaps—of the nature of the artist and the role of the intellectual. In two important documents of 1948, which argue the case for De Gaulle, and develop in explicit ideological terms the findings of the *Psychology of Art*, Malraux signals the death of nineteenth-century liberalism and proposes a new kind of 'liberal hero'.[21] It is necessary, he claims, to separate once and for all cultural from political liberalism. Despite an unprecedented internationalization of culture, the political myth of internationalism is in its death-throes. The heart of that myth was that the less a man was bound to his country, the more man he became. Now it is clear that in becoming (say) less French he simply becomes more Russian. The reason for this is not the dialectical march of history but the ruthless development of propaganda techniques directed towards the destruction of Man's freedom of thought, and the creative freedom implicit in Europe's cultural past.

Malraux goes on to reject neutrality in politics for the sake of the autonomy of culture and the quality of mind it implies. Although America and Russia have both exploited Man through propaganda techniques, the incidence of the former is mainly limited to the economic field. America, moreover, has always looked to European art with respect: in fact, Europe and America, in terms of culture, are not apart but belong to what Malraux calls Atlantic civilization. The artists of this civilization have shown that genius consists in 'a difference conquered', not in difference cultivated for its own sake, or yet in an abolition of individual difference.

The liberal hero is, in this light, intellectual or artist capable of political action to preserve man's free access to his cultural heritage, but also capable of withdrawal from action when this end is achieved. Malraux himself practised such a temporary sacrifice of the intellect more than once. His political career is absolutely logical —if that is what one looks for in politics. It is easily shown that his views have changed in accord with the principle that politics should always serve culture rather than culture politics. His switch from Communism, or near-Communism, to de Gaulle simply maintains, to his mind, the ultimacy of culture. In 1933 'the task was to open in Moscow the libraries which were being burnt in Berlin', but in 1948: 'the condemnation of Picasso in Moscow . . . seeks to be a defence of the five-year plans'.

Contemporary France has become the proving grounds for the question whether the political and intellectual foundations of humanism can be reconstructed. How may cultural liberalism be sustained in the face of political exigencies? Is Malraux's liberal hero (who revives the myth of Cincinnatus and Lawrence of Arabia) [22] an ideal capable of realization? One is struck by the either/or assumptions put forward between 1918 and 1940: Geneva or Moscow, America or Moscow, Order or Anarchy, Intellect or Action, East or West, Tradition or the Individual Talent, Romanticism or Classicism. . . . The wonderland (or wasteland) philosophy of humanism, which tried to crowd as many rooms as possible into its house, and courageously held to the notion of the unity of Man, finds itself continually challenged by new forms of dualism. All writers in those precarious years sought a new simplicity, some escape from the decay of humanistic thought into historicist eclecticism, some proof that Man is more than a curiosity shop in limbo and the intellectual more than a fickle clerk. The question that confronted Malraux was what reconstruction of the idea of Man could issue from the literary acts of past and present. Between the two wars all Europe was involved: today France alone seems destined to suffer a clash of attitudes which must either destroy or transform humanistic ideals.

The role of the historian, it has been said, is to overcome history by history, and only in this sense are the *Psychology of Art* and Malraux's novels historically minded. The great antagonist of his heroes, whether adventurers or artists, is always time. They feel themselves alienated from the present tense, from the 'here and now' vanishing with hegelian speed into the 'there and then' of history, but a history no longer explicable in hegelian or religious terms as proceeding by trial towards salvation. Perhaps this is also the simplest way of interpreting Malraux's foredoomed insistence on present tense and first person in his earliest novel, as well as his later, more hopeful emphasis on the *presence* of all great art, however far from us in culture or time. That speed of translating political events into art, which reappears in the thematic texture of his work as the too quickness of death or fate or simply of the world to the senses, shows a mind haunted by the problem of overcoming time within time. His mode of structural repetition, which suggests a sublime if monotonous eternal recurrence, the rapid replacement of one fatality by another and the complex idea of Man's conspiracy with his fate point to the secret essence of *fiction*, a realm in which Man becomes the giver of the given. Art reveals his powers to antedate experience: even time is within Man's purview, a flame which the moth creates for itself, the cause of its death but also the substance of its life. The question is never that of a deliverance from time but that of its possession. Just as Psyche or Antigone trespassed on Aphrodite's realm to make love the property of mankind, so Fate, perhaps, is simply the god of Time, and Malraux's 'conquerors' trespass on the last and most sacred realm of all.

NOTES

1. Cf. the illusion of the sleeping body turning into a corpse, and below, pp. 62–64.

2. 'Dostojewskij', *Der Russische Realismus in der Weltliteratur* (Berlin, 1952).

3. See his preface to Roger Stéphane's *Portrait de l'Aventurier* (Paris, 1950).

4. Marcel Arland in 'Un nouveau "Mal du Siècle"', originally published in 1924. It is translated in *From the N.R.F.*, Justin O'Brien ed. (New York, 1958), pp. 28–38.

5. See *L'Etranger* and *La Peste*. Many of Thomas Mann's characters pass through a similar kind of conspiratorial blindness to the nature of the 'plague'; e.g. Aschenbach in 'Death in Venice', the narrator of 'Mario and the Magician', the inhabitants of the Magic Mountain. . . .

6. *Ecrits*, 'Les Cahiers Verts 70' (Paris, 1927). The search for Death is the theme of Malraux's earliest piece of fiction, a fantasy entitled *Lunes en Papier* (1921).

7. It may not be without significance that Hemmelrich and Clappique make their escape by adopting an utterly strange identity—when the latter, disguised as a sailor, catches sight of himself in a mirror, he momentarily does not recognize himself.

8. It is easy to overinterpret Malraux's elliptical detail, but does not Tchen's inability to share stand in strange contrast to Katov's 'sharing' of the cyanide, which is really a not-sharing, a sacrifice?

9. *Lunes en Papier* (1921) and *Royaume Farfelu* (1928). Reasons of space prevent their consideration here. The theme of both is related to that of the mock or Pyrrhic victory: the haste to do something which involves the destruction of the doer or a triumph proving useless.

10. See above, pp. 45 ff. The helpless witnessing of death remains, however, a major principle of structure, though the dead belong now often to the younger, and the witnesses to the older generation.

11. The pilot who flies Kassner to Prague 'descends' into a storm even as the latter had 'descended' to prison; the altimeter of the plane, plunging to get under the storm, registers in reverse (1000, 950, 920 . . . 600, 500, 4 . . .) Kassner's counting to 10 and to 100 so as to 'get in under' the guard's return step, one of the prison-games by which he fought his increasing sense of the irremediable; when climbing the stairs of his home in Prague he fears to find himself back in prison, for his suffering had begun by climbing the stairs into a fellow Communist's apartment; and the book ends with a descent into an 'earthly' night that seeks to purge his previous 'unearthly' descents: 'All this would become a part of life, a stairway they would descend side by side, steps in the street. . . .'

12. This episode, which occurs only in part II, points to the symphonic rather than linear construction of the novel.

13. This novel, first published in Switzerland in 1943, is the surviving part of *La Lutte avec L'Ange*, a larger work destroyed by Nazis.

13a. The setting soon changes, however, to an open field, and this movement from a closed and 'artificial' to an open and 'natural' space is repeated in other sections of the novel.

14. For a complete listing, see the bibliography. Although I have consulted all of Malraux's writings on art, I have preferred to take my quotations (unless otherwise stated) from *The Psychology of Art*, tr. Stuart Gilbert (New York, 1949–50). Short excerpts of a sentence or less may come from a different work without being specifically mentioned.

15. The view Malraux popularizes is variously stressed long before him. A historical placing cannot be attempted here. But the conscious, even dogmatic revolt against *vraisemblance* began before the fine practice, if groping theory, of the Impressionists: it exists in full vociferous bloom in the writings of Blake, not mentioned by Malraux either as painter or poet. German art historians, such as Riegl, Worringer and Dvorak, anticipated Malraux at many points, especially in the theory of a 'will to art' (*Kunstwollen*). But the richest parallels for his point of view are literary. The Romantic poets are clearly its tumultuous fountainhead, and this is made finely obvious by Northrop Frye's *Anatomy of Criticism* (Princeton, 1957), which in some respects, stands to the study of literature as Malraux's *Psychology* to the study of art. The farther literary background of the theory is illumined by M. H. Abrams, *The Mirror and the Lamp* (New York, 1953), pp. 272–85, 'The Poem as Heterocosm'. In France the constellation Baudelaire–Mallarmé–Valéry (see especially the latter's 'Introduction to the Method of Leonardo da Vinci') was the main bearer of the idea, and today literary theorists closest to Malraux are Gaston Bachelard and Maurice Blanchot. Malraux's own application of the antimimetic view to literature finds its richest source in his marginal annotations to Gaëtan Picon's *Malraux par lui-même* (Paris, 1953).

16. The above discussion and quotations are drawn from *La Metamorphose des Dieux* (Paris, 1957). Malraux's 'sacrosanct' (*le sacré*) practically coincides with Rudolf Otto's 'Das Heilige'.

17. Valéry terms all composition *l'arbitraire raisonné*, a view shared by modern criticism, which attributes to every good work of art an inherent if, in some sense, arbitrary logic. Cf. also Poe's 'The Philosophy of Composition'.

18. Preface to the *Phenomenology of the Spirit*, tr. J. B. Baillie.

19. 'Replies to 13 Questions', *Partisan Review*, XXII, no. 2 (Spring 1955), 157–70.

20. This phrase, 'l'horreur lucide de la séduction', is originally used in *La Tentation de l'Occident*. Malraux also calls it a 'negative classicism'.

21. *The Case for De Gaulle*. A dialogue between André Malraux and James Burnham (New York, 1949); 'Postface' (1948) to *The Conquerors*, tr. for the Beacon Paperback edition (Boston, 1956).

22. Lawrence refused to assume power in Damascus, afraid that even a few days of it might change him radically. He returned from conflict with Man to that ordinary struggle with the world of things which Malraux has always considered a most important ingredient of the West's greatness.

BIOGRAPHICAL DATES

Precise details and dates concerning Malraux are rather scarce because of his reticence. I give here a minimum of information about which we are reasonably sure.

1901   Born at Paris, 3 November. Education at the Lycée Condorcet and the Ecole des Langues Orientales.

1923–25 Trips to Indo-China. He helps the Kuomintang in some role, possibly as commissary for propaganda.

1933   *La Condition Humaine* wins the *Prix Goncourt*. Malraux has been busy with various archaeological expeditions and is an editor for the Gallimard publishing house.

1934   President of the World Committee for the liberation of Dimitroff and Thaelmann. Together with Gide delivers a petition to Hitler. Visits Moscow.

1936   Plays a leading role in organizing and commanding Foreign aviation in the Spanish Civil War. After being wounded comes to America to raise funds for the Republican cause.

1939   Joins Tank Corps as a private, is wounded, taken prisoner, and escapes to carry on for the Resistance.

1944   As Colonel Berger, Commanding Officer
        of the Alsace-Lorraine Brigade.
        Wounded, made prisoner, rescued by
        his men.

1945   Minister for Information in De Gaulle's
        first, short-lived administration.

1948   A chief spokesman for De Gaulle on his
        return to public life.

1958–59 At first Minister for Information in De
        Gaulle's Government; now Minister
        for Cultural Affairs.

BIBLIOGRAPHY

A. Works of Fiction: *Lunes en Papier* (1921); *La Tentation de l'Occident* (1926); *Royaume Farfelu* (1928); *Les Conquérants* (1928); *La Voie Royale* (1930); *La Condition Humaine* (1933); *Le Temps du Mépris* (1935); *L'Espoir* (1937); *Les Noyers de l'Altenburg* (1943).

B. Works on Art and selected miscellaneous writings (* indicates works which have been translated):

'D'une Jeunesse Européenne', *Ecrits* (Les Cahier Verts) 1927.

'Réponse à Léon Trotsky,' *Nouvelle Révue Française*, No. 211 (April, 1931), pp. 501–7.

* 'Préface', *L'Amant de Lady Chatterley*, by D. H. Lawrence. Gallimard, 1932.

* 'Préface', *Sanctuaire*, by William Faulkner. Gallimard, 1933.

'Préface', *Indochine S.O.S.*, by Andrée Viollis. Gallimard, 1935.

* 'Réponse aux 64', *Commune*, No. 27 (December 1935), pp. 410–16.

'Laclos', in *Tableau de la Littérature Française*, Gallimard, 1939, pp. 417–28.

'Préface', '. . . qu'une larme dans l'océan', by Manes Sperber. Calman-Lévy, 1952.

The Case for De Gaulle. A dialogue between

André Malraux and James Burnham. Random House, 1949.

    * 'Postface', *Les Conquérants*. Grasset, 1949.

Esquisse d'une Psychologie du Cinéma. Gallimard, 1949.

    * *Dessins de Goya au musée de Prado*. Geneva: Skira, 1947.

    * *La Psychologie de l'Art*. Geneva: Skira, 1947–50.

    * *Saturne*. Gallimard, 1950.

    * *Les Voix du Silence*. Gallimard, 1951.

Vermeer de Delft. Gallimard, 1952.

Le Musée Imaginaire de la Sculpture Mondiale. Gallimard, 1952–54.

Des Bas-reliefs aux Grottes Sacrées. Gallimard, 1954.

Le Monde Chrétien. Gallimard, 1954.

La Métamorphose des Dieux. Gallimard, 1957.

C. Translations:

    (i) Fiction—

        The Conquerors, tr. W. S. Whale. New York, 1929; Beacon Paperback reprint, 1956.

        The Royal Way, tr. Stuart Gilbert. New York, 1935.

        Man's Fate, tr. H. M. Chevalier. New York, 1934. Also published in England as *Storm in Shanghai*, tr. Alistair Mac-Donald. London, 1934.

        Days of Contempt (in America, *Days of Wrath*), tr. H. M. Chevalier. London, 1936.

Days of Hope (in America, *Man's Hope*), tr. Stuart Gilbert and Alistair MacDonald. London and New York, 1938.

The Walnut Trees of Altenburg, tr. A. W. Fielding. London, 1952.

(ii) Works on Art and miscellaneous writings—

Preface to Faulkner's *Sanctuary: Yale French Studies* No. 10 (1952), 92–94.

Preface to *Lady Chatterley's Lover: Yale French Studies* No. 11 (1953), 55–58; also in *From the NRF*, ed. Justin O'Brien, New York, 1958, pp. 194–98.

Rejoinder to the 64: *Yale French Studies* No. 18 (1957), 28–30. Our Cultural Heritage: *Ibid.* 30–38.

Postface to *The Conquerors:* Beacon Paperback edition (1956), pp. 175–93. (Postface trans. J. LeClerq).

Goya drawings from the Prado, tr. E. Sackville-West, London, 1947.

The Psychology of Art, tr. Stuart Gilbert. New York, 1949–50.

The Voices of Silence, tr. Stuart Gilbert. New York, 1953.

Saturn, An essay on Goya, tr. C. W. Chilton. New York, 1957.

'Lawrence and the Demon of the Absolute.' *Hudson Review*, VIII (1956), 519–32.

D. On Malraux: There are two full-scale studies in English, W. M. Frohock, *André Malraux and the Tragic Imagination*, Stanford, 1952, and E. Gannon, S. J., *The Honour of Being a Man*, Chicago, 1957. Of the numerous articles on Malraux the following should not escape notice. Edmund Wilson, 'André Malraux', in *The Shores of Light*; A Literary Chronicle of the Twenties and Thirties, New York, pp. 566–74. This is a review of *La Condition Humaine* originally published in *The New Republic*, and has an interesting reply of Malraux's appended. Also Wilson's 'Malraux and Silone', *The New Yorker* of 8 September, 1945, pp. 74–8. Nicola Chiaromonte, 'Malraux and the Demons of Action', *The Partisan Review*, XV (1948), pp. 776–89 and 912–23. Henri Peyre, *The Contemporary French Novel*, New York, 1957, pp. 182–215. Janet Flanner, *Men and Monuments*, New York, 1957, pp. 1–70. Irving Howe, *Politics and the Novel*, New York, 1957, pp. 203–17. R. B. Lewis, *The Picaresque Saint*, New York, 1959, pp. 275–295. The most compact little study published in France, and containing fine marginal annotations by Malraux is Gaëtan Picon's *Malraux par lui-même*, Paris, 1953. *Yale French Studies* No. 18 (1957) is entirely devoted to Malraux.